From the Other Side of the Couch

A BIBLICAL COUNSELOR'S GUIDE TO
RELATIONAL LIVING

Judy Lair, LPCC

Sarah,
Truth = Freedom
I loved spending time with you!
I hope you find joy + happiness.
Judy

All references to clients are anonymous and any identifiable information has been changed to protect confidentiality.

Judy A. Lair, LPCC
Counselorplace LLC
6827 N. High Street, Suite 121
Worthington, OH 43085
www.counselorplace.com

Afghan & pillow made by Aunt Goldie & Cousin Randa
Cover photos and interior graphics by Tabitha Stone
Make-up by Mitchell Westfall

Feel free to contact Judy Lair regarding speaking engagements.

Contents

Introduction: *Hello!*.. *1*

1. From the Counseling Couch to the Therapist's Chair 5

2. What's Love Got To Do With It? 25

   Models of Relationship 25

   Barriers to Living the Relational Model 31

3. How Did It Go Wrong? 47

   Why Are We Here? 47

   In the Beginning 50

   Outcome-Based Model 57

4. The Transformation Process 67

   Barriers to Transformation 68

   Stages of Transformation 71

   Transformation in Narnia 75

ROADMAP TO FREEDOM

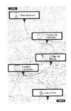

5. Woundedness 89

    How We Are Wounded.. 90

    Compartmentalization 94

    Coping Strategies 104

    Become as a Little Child 106

6. Processing Emotions 111

    Permission 112

    Information and Energy.. 113

    Garden of Gethsemane 116

    Fixing Feelings... 120

    Grieving.. 123

    God's Timing 125

7. Critiquing Beliefs 131

    Beliefs About Ourselves... 133

    Beliefs About Others 137

    Beliefs About God 144

8. Truthful Confession 151

    Freedom Thru Truth.. 153

    Agreeing with God 154

Truth in the Midst of a Storm...157

9. Living Free 171

Seeing Yourself Clearly 172

Don't Settle for Better, Reach for Great...................176

Name Change..180

Seeing Life Through the Lens of Relationship..........182

Joyful Living...186

REFERENCES 191

Thanks

To God the Father, Jesus, and the Holy Spirit for loving and caring for me well and for teaching me to love myself and others well.

To my wonderful clients who have allowed me to walk alongside them for a season.

To my son Ben for giving me grace when I was in the midst of my healing season.

To my mentor who pursued me, guided me, and shared with me the biblical relational principles that are the basis of my life and practice.

In the book of life, the answers aren't in the back.

—CHARLIE BROWN

The Swing

Once upon a time, a long while ago, I sat
upon a swing. One push would launch me
toward heaven above, I'd take flight on my
sunbeam wings. There were no limits to
the size of my dreams, for the sky was
wide and vast. Suspended in time and
freed from earth's bounds, my vision for the future I did
cast. I want to sing songs of praise to you, Lord, and pen sweet
words of love; to cause men's hearts to seek the truth, which can
only be found in You above.

Once upon a time, just yesterday, I again sat upon a swing.
Contemplating my ride through life 'tis true, I'd let go of my dreams.
My limitless vision, where did it go? My heart had turned to stone.
My feet were dragging in confusion and doubt. My fears had left
me all alone. God had passed me by, used someone else. There's
no vision left for me. I'd live out my days, just sitting here, hidden
in obscurity.

Once upon a time, at this moment now, I sit upon a swing. I now
understand that I have the choice to accept what the Father will
bring. I realize now I can only see a tiny piece of the sky. I cannot
grasp the whole of God's plan, even when I swing way up high. By
faith I begin to swing again, and even dream a bit; of poems and
people and musical notes and how God can make everything fit.

Hello!

Welcome to my counseling office, let me know if I can get you a glass of water or cup of coffee. I'll sit in my forest green arm chair next to the lamp stand with photos of my son. You can curl up on the couch across from me. If you're cold, go ahead and grab the afghan my aunt Goldie made to cover your lap. Now let's talk.

Clients have asked me for years to write a book that sounds like the conversations we have in my office every day. This is not your typical self-help book with tips and tools to help you manage difficult situations. I do a little bit of that, but mainly I focus on principles. Every counseling session focuses on how transforming your heart, mind, and character leads to healing and happiness. In this book you will read a lot about viewpoint, because that makes a difference in getting clarity and seeing truth. We live in a complicated world and the enemy loves to use confusion and doubt to deceive. I strive to sit in God's living room looking at life through his vantage point and sharing that perspective with clients.

Every client that walks into my office and every person who picks up this book is looking for hope. Hope that change is possible this time, wondering if they are too broken to be fixed. What I can tell you is that I absolutely, positively, completely believe in God's heart for you and your healing -- because I now know His heart for me. God loves you with the same passion I experience. The process I share shows you how to identify and wrestle with the barriers that keep you from receiving and experiencing that same truth. I invite you to be open to the concepts I share and have lots of discussions with God about them. Whether you agree or disagree with me is not as important as what you gain in the conversation process.

I've structured the book as if we're talking in my office. First, I'll introduce myself. I expect that you, like me, are very particular about who you allow to speak into your life. Every counselor has their own views on how relationship dysfunction happens and how to address it. This view is based on their training and personal experiences. It's important for clients to decide if the counselor's framework is the best vehicle to get them where they want to go. For that reason, I purposefully share my background and the key life experiences that form my beliefs. I've done my best to be transparent, allowing you to get a feel for my heart, character, and motives.

Second, I'll explain the general principles I rely on related to beliefs, feelings, thoughts, actions, etc. Principles such as learning what it means to love ourselves and others in a godly way, why we need to go back and open up old painful scars, and how learning new skills such as grieving can draw us closer to God and each other. After discussing the foundational principles, I'll introduce a counseling model I developed called the Roadmap to Freedom. Walking out this journey takes you from a place of woundedness to a life lived out of joy. Each chapter moves you step by step along in the process. I've made this journey myself and am honored to walk alongside to guide and encourage you.

One of the things you will learn about me is that I see themes and lessons everywhere. Jesus taught new concepts by using parables to illustrate his points. I, too, like to use common cultural illustrations. You will see me using metaphors, parallels, references to biblical accounts, books, and even movie references to get a concept across. Clients tell me this approach really helps them to retain what we talk about in session.

Third, you will find examples of what the transformation process looks like through stories from my own life and client accounts. (Yes, I have changed client names and identifying information.) Reading someone else's story gives us the ability to see ourselves more clearly since it's often hard to see the survival mechanisms we've used for years. These self-protective beliefs and instinctual responses were necessary in childhood, but now make it hard to live a fulfilling adult life. Together, we will ask God to bring you context, clarity, compassion, and understanding about the pain and hurt you've experienced and their impact on your present life.

I love talking about developing a relational "one another" approach where folks open up and are vulnerable with each other for the purpose of sharing, caring, and teaching. By interacting with the concepts in this book, you are opening your heart to me and giving God permission to show you truth. Such a journey is exciting and also sobering. Jesus cautioned the disciples to count the cost when deciding whether to follow him. Undergoing a transformative journey where God reveals truth about yourself and others will impact every facet of your life -- but isn't that what you were hoping for when you picked up this book?

> *Knowing can be a curse on a person's life. I'd traded in a pack of lies for a pack of truth, and I didn't know which one was heavier. Which one took the most strength to carry around? It was a ridiculous question, though, because once you know the truth, you can't ever go back and pick up your suitcase of lies. Heavier or not, the truth is yours now. (Kid, p. 255)*

So, once again, welcome to my office. There are tissues on the little black table next to the window by the couch. Some days we will laugh together as I tell you the latest dumb thing I said or did. Other times my heart will groan for the pain you've experienced and the tears you are shedding. What's for certain is that God will always be with us as we walk along your unique transformative journey together.

CHAPTER 1

From the Counseling Couch to the Therapist's Chair

I never dreamed of being a counselor. I never lined my dolls up and solved their problems. I wasn't the one all my friends came to when they needed advice or a shoulder to cry on. I never even thought much about therapists, good or bad, until my early 20s when I needed someone to talk to about problems with my friends and family. At that time, the idea of paying someone to listen to me vent seemed ridiculous, but there didn't seem to be a better option. Counseling turned out to be very helpful as the therapist normalized and validated my feelings, helping me understand myself.

In my late 30s, I found myself struggling with more issues and difficult decisions. This was frustrating since I've always been independent and could find a way to push through, but this time was different. Admitting I needed help was embarrassing and demoralizing. That's when I looked in the mirror and saw someone I didn't know and wasn't sure I liked. Feeling like I was going to explode, I humbled myself and once again walked into a counselor's office. That decision changed the course of my life.

On the client side of the couch, I spent a lot of time learning how to let God reveal me to me. Seems like it should be a straightforward task. Actually, it's an amazingly complicated, wondrous process filled with fear and excitement. Kind of like Horton's journey in the Dr.

Seuss' book *Horton Hears a Who!* Horton heard a small speck of dust talk to him, but no one believed him. When the dust speck was stolen, Horton went on a difficult journey to get it back. Along the way he was heckled by jungle animals for his belief. He had a crisis of faith as to whether he could believe in his own experience. Horton decided he would rather be wrong in choosing to believe in himself than live a life filled with second guessing. This strength of character allowed Horton to withstand persecution when he was taken prisoner and the dust speck was about to be destroyed.

I believe God is always talking to us in a still, small voice about who He created us to be. Experiencing disappointment, hurt, and pain in childhood causes us to put on protective armor that drowns out God's voice. When we begin to shed the armor, there's often push back from those around us and our own fear that we won't like who is underneath.

About a year into therapy the second time, God started whispering in my ear about becoming a counselor. I'd be sitting on the couch talking about deep emotional things with my therapist and hear, *"You can do this too. I created you to help people in this same way."* I was flabbergasted and completely rejected such a crazy suggestion. I'd argue with God, throwing out silly excuses about not being warm and fuzzy or not having enough patience to listen to someone who was as messed up as me. The truth was that I was used to living in fear. Believing God meant being vulnerable and potentially letting clients down if I didn't have answers for their very real, painful problems. I had worked very hard to stay in my comfort zone, feeling competent and safe. Stepping out of that zone into relationships with hurting people would be scary and messy. I'd risk feeling like a failure.

This is the moment when my self-protective mechanisms launched an assault. When the goal in life is to keep bad stuff out, our threat assessment analysis is distorted. The viewpoint here is important. When we step out to follow God, there will be situations out of our control and we will feel like we've failed. But God isn't all that concerned with mistakes during our earth internship. When we take a relational risk, we learn more about us. At the same time, God gives the other person an opportunity to learn about Him. It's a win-win situation all around. If all we care about is not making a mistake, we will never put ourselves in a situation to learn anything important.

Much of my life was spent searching for the key to joy and happiness. I would hear a sermon and try my best to be Christ-like, but like my attempts at dieting, it only lasted a day or two. Then I would beat myself up for not being perfect, decide I needed to try something else, and go to a new conference or read a new book only to start the cycle again. No matter how much I wanted to live a happy, fulfilled life, I was always disappointed in myself.

> Why was I born? What was valuable about me? Did God really love me, or even like me? How do I find God's will for my life? How do I turn the other cheek and when do I get to be the one who's loved?

My counselor suggested the answers would be found by viewing the movie of my life and asking God to show me important themes. These themes would hold clues as to who God created me to be and how I had lost sight of those truths.

Born in Boise, Idaho, we lived in Nampa, Idaho until I was 7. I'm the oldest, my sister Wanda is 18 months younger, Karla is 5 years younger, and my brother Jeff is the youngest. My mom, Iverna, was a teacher and my dad, Allen, managed a gas station. We had plenty of relatives nearby from both sides of the family.

My favorite childhood memories were the family gatherings at my maternal grandma and grandpa's house. We kids would be running around out by the barn or down by the creek. Everybody would take a turn on the manual ice cream machine hand crank. This is where I inherited my love of singing. After dinner, all the instruments would come out and the hymn sing would begin. Piano, guitar, banjo, accordion, flute, and me standing on top of the coffee table singing my heart out. I can still hear echoes of *"I'll Fly Away"* in four part harmony.

I began singing in church while in elementary school after moving to Camrose, Alberta, Canada. Every Sunday, a different church in town would broadcast their service on the radio. When it was our Sunday to host, I'd often be asked to sing a solo. I was a petite, blue-eyed gal with white-blonde wavy hair who was too short to reach the microphone on the pulpit. Someone had to bring a box up for me to stand on to be seen and heard.

Living in Canada was great for a kid. Camrose was surrounded by lots of fields and many of our church families were farmers. It started snowing in October and each successive snow added to the layers that lasted until April. We built forts in the front yard where the snow drifts were taller than me. When I got older, I drove a snowmobile down the back alley to the gas station and then rode through the fields all afternoon. Our church youth group had amazing sledding parties. We'd take a snowmobile up the hill and slide down on an inner tube to the bonfire below. There was always lots of hot chocolate and laughter. As a youngster, being seen as a "good girl" was very important. I tried to listen and obey well. In middle school I joined my school's safety patrol crossing guard. I loved my neon orange uniform belt and the red stop sign that gave me power over traffic.

We moved to Hershey, Pennsylvania when I was 13 years old. When I tried out for the 8th grade choir, the teacher asked me to sing *The Star Spangled Banner* and I didn't know it, so I sang *God Save The Queen* instead. People walking by the choir room stuck their heads in to see who was singing in a Canadian accent. My parents bought me a guitar and I'd sit in my bedroom writing songs, learning how to play

'70s and '80s ballads, tearfully singing Donny Osmond songs about puppy love.

I remember always feeling like an outsider, especially in the middle of a group of peers. Being an overachiever with an introverted personality style, a critical eye for detail, and a high level of intuition made it very difficult for me to let my guard down. Even when I accepted invitations and joined my friends in activities, I never felt connected.

The summer after moving to Pennsylvania I begged my parents to let me go on a Teen Missions summer ministry trip. At 14 years of age, I was the youngest member of a group of kids and staff members who traveled by bus for three weeks across the United States and Canada. We drove to national parks and set up camp. During the day we witnessed about Jesus to anyone who would talk to us. In the evening we would sing and preach around a campfire. Traveling with strangers was one of the hardest things I've ever done in my life. My shyness made it hugely difficult to do evangelism. I was an easy target. We stopped at a church near the Gulf of Mississippi for a weekend and headed for the beach. I still cringe with embarrassment at how the older girls made fun of my hairy legs. Girls know where and how to trigger the self-hatred knife. I'd often sit on top of the suitcases in the back of the bus, alone, wishing I could get away from everyone.

Looking at my teenage years now in retrospect, a clear emerges that I believed I was different from everyone else. The more that belief was reinforced, the more I shut down and distanced myself from others. My idea of the perfect Christian was an outgoing extrovert who shared her faith easily, never got scared or anxious, loved everyone, and could quote the perfect Bible verse for any occasion. I, certainly, was not that person.

Church was really important to me. I knew I loved God, but always felt like God was disappointed in me because I wasn't being a good enough Christian. That belief was reinforced at Bible conferences where they gave us step-by-step instructions on how to find and live out God's will. But it was never that simple for me because I always questioned everything. I've never been one to just accept someone's word, even if they were my parent, teacher, or pastor. I've always needed to wrestle with beliefs for myself. Since no one else seemed to have questions, I concluded I was weird and got the sense many people considered me to be a "drama queen."

Aunt Goldie was the one person I knew who always loved me exactly the way I was. She loved to hear me talk about anything and everything while puttering around in her strawberry-themed kitchen. Strawberry kitchen towels, ceramic strawberries on her counters, strawberry cookie jar, refrigerator magnets -- you name it! In Idaho, Aunt Goldie and Uncle Randall lived on a small farm with horses. When they moved to Bakersfield, California, there was a huge tortoise living in her backyard. During family visits, we kids would ride it like a horse. I last visited her in 1998 at her home in McMinnville, Oregon. We sat in her kitchen and, once again, it felt like I was 7 years old. I loved sharing with Aunt Goldie and Cousin Randa all my big dreams about who I wanted to be and what I wanted to do when I grew up.

In 1974 as a sophomore, I went on a high school trip to England. After the excruciating group experience in 8th grade, I desperately wanted to blend in with the other students. I tried alcohol for the first time and allowed myself to go much too far physically with a boy. These experiences created so much shame that I couldn't even look at the trip photos for more than 10 years. I talked with my youth group leaders when I returned, but couldn't ever shake the disgust I felt about myself and my choices. I mistakenly believed it was a sign of my terrible character. I know now my actions came out of a belief that I was unlovable.

A few years later I was a freshman at Northwest Nazarene College in Nampa, Idaho. I hoped the change in environment would bring about a change in me. Unfortunately, all the same old patterns resurfaced. I continued to be an introvert pretending to be an extrovert. My roommate could totally tell I was faking it and she kept me at a distance. The girls on my floor spent time with a floor of freshman guys. At times I was included, but usually only when they wanted an errand girl or tutor. All these observations reinforced the belief that I was messed up. Coming home to Hershey for the summer, I truly believed no guy would ever like me for me.

The summer between my freshman and sophomore years I returned home to Hershey and worked at Hersheypark as the Stroller Rental attendant. I also took a second job working third shift as a waitress. A short order cook named Rick paid me lots of attention. Rick was the opposite of what my Christian parents wanted for their daughter. He didn't attend church, drank, smoked, and slept around. Rick laughed at my naivety when I asked why a male customer would leave me a large tip with his business card.

At the end of that summer, I tried to forget Rick and transferred to George Fox College in Newberg, Oregon so I could room with my cousin Julie. Maybe living in the same room with someone that I knew loved me would help me love myself. I ended up with mono and had to leave school and returned home to Hershey.

At the age of 19, I felt like a hopeless disappointment to myself and to God. I had tried as hard as I could to do all the "right" things, but I didn't feel any happier and life wasn't any easier. When Rick came along, he offered me attention and liked who I was without needing me to change. It seemed easier to settle for Rick than to keep failing God and everyone else. A year later we got married and a black pit opened up in my soul. I stopped going to church and distanced myself from family and old friends. I began working as a paralegal for a company that operated adult education training schools across the country. We would hold meetings at the headquarters in Harrisburg. Many of the school directors took full advantage of being away from home to go out with staff and party. Rick and CareerCom introduced me to a brand new world where I could bury my head in the sand rather than face my disappointment.

A couple years into the marriage, Rick had a bad fall at work and spent the next two years at home on workers comp for a back injury. If Rick turned or moved the wrong way, it pinched a nerve in his back causing his legs to give out. Several times at home, and once while at a restaurant, Rick's back flared up and I needed help to get him to the hospital. Twice, neighbors called an ambulance after finding Rick laying in the front yard. On arrival at the ER, the doctors gave Rick muscle relaxers and pain medication. After a few hours, the nerves calmed down and Rick was sent home. It felt like all the responsibility of keeping our lives intact fell on me. I had to make sure I kept my job so we could make ends meet, but many times I spent hours in the ER with Rick, getting only a few hours of sleep before heading into work.

Rick was sent to a pain clinic in Baltimore, Maryland for several weeks to try and stabilize his lumbar spine. The doctors put a body cast around Rick's torso to allow time for the bone to strengthen. I'd make the 2½ hour drive to visit every weekend while continuing to keep the wheels on the bus in our daily life. Depression set in. I found myself being easily irritated, having less patience, problems concentrating with no energy or motivation. I was angry at our situation and upset at myself for being angry with my injured husband. Those complicated feelings prompted my first visit to a counselor. She normalized my feelings in light of the circumstances and gave me permission to be angry without feeling guilty. I had every right to hate how Rick's health problems caused my life to be stressful, lonely, chaotic, and heavy. I learned being angry with someone did not mean I didn't love them, nor did it mean I was selfish.

Rick eventually underwent surgery where they took bone from his hip and grafted it over the weak spot in his lumbar spine. He finally returned to work, but our marriage continued to crumble. In counseling for the first time, I started learning how to be truthful about my feelings and to look at the ways I lied to myself. It was true I agreed to marry Rick because I believed I had sinned by giving him my virginity and getting married was my penance. But I got into the relationship in the first place because I didn't believe in my own worth and value.

Seven years later, I couldn't hide how much I hated my life. Rick continued to be a carefree, immature guy who had no idea how to be good for me. We had two very different foundations and life strategies. I tried to talk to him about how I felt, but it was as if we were speaking foreign languages. My depression symptoms intensified and I seriously questioned whether I wanted to live or die. Those thoughts scared me into action. Desperate and isolated, I decided there was no hope of finding out what was true about me if I stayed in the marriage and I asked for a divorce.

My guilt over the divorce was unbearable. I knew I had hurt Rick and didn't know how to make amends, yet knew I could not be married to him or I would drown emotionally and harm myself physically. Lost, I didn't know which direction to go to find myself or God. I shared my feelings about the divorce with some coworkers and found them to be encouraging and supportive -- especially a single, male school director from Columbus, Ohio. I had met Lewis several times when he came to the home office. He was always polite and treated me with respect. I soaked up his words of praise for my hard work and good character. When he proposed, I accepted and moved to Columbus, Ohio in 1988.

Looking back now, I can see how broken I was as a person. I remember thinking, "This is the last chance I have for anyone to love me, so I'd better take it." I knew for sure I could bring good things into Lewis's life. What I didn't know was that subconsciously, I was trying to work out emotional issues with my dad through Lewis. Research shows we choose a version of the opposite gender parent in our romantic relationships, trying to resolve the outstanding emotional issues with that parent. When daughters don't receive everything God created us to get from our fathers, we look to other males to fill those holes. Sons often think their wife is completely opposite from their mother, later to realize the outside was different but the inside was the same.

The next 10 years I worked hard at providing a happy home for Lewis. Our son Ben was born in 1989 and I loved being a mom. I recently transferred old home movies to DVDs. Watching the DVDs brought back wonderful memories. Mother Goose came to Ben's 4th birthday party and told stories. Several birthday parties were held at the roller skating rink with his friends. There were baseball and basketball games, Christmas choirs, and band concerts. It was really fun to go back and watch Ben and his best friend Seton write their letters to Santa. I loved watching the boys dump out their bags of Halloween candy and negotiate trades of favorite treats.

I did my best to care for Lewis and to find things outside the house I enjoyed. But there was always a nagging voice saying I wasn't being truthful and I couldn't keep up the charade forever. Avoiding that voice, I put a lot of energy into becoming really good at my job as a paralegal at the law firm. Needing to hear I was a valuable employee, I worked hard to become indispensable and make sure the reassurance kept coming. Although I handled all types of litigation, I became a specialist at personal injury cases. I met with injured clients, educated them on the legal process, gathered all the necessary records, and drafted documents for insurance companies and courts. Not surprisingly, my favorite part was helping clients go through what I now know were the stages of grief. Looking back, it's interesting to see how God was already preparing me for a change of career!

Church was another area where I received validation that kept me afloat. Although Lewis never attended, I would take Ben to church with me and often helped out in the nursery. I've always had a special bond with babies. I think kids know I look at them as people, not simply as children. Since I was a teen, I've loved to rock and sing babies to sleep. One Sunday I was holding an extremely tired little guy who was fighting sleep with all his might. He cried and squirmed, refusing to close his eyes until he suddenly gave up and his entire body went limp as he slept. That incident is a great illustration of how we adults wrestle with God. We argue, cry, yell, and wrestle with God when circumstances are hard, but it's His hope that eventually we'll surrender fully to the truth that God loves us at all times and in all situations.

Ten years into marriage with Lewis all the legs of the stool I was sitting on gave way and I crashed into a deep depression. My marriage, my faith, and my job all crumbled at the same time. I'd been recruited to become the office manager at a prolife Christian ministry. Shortly after taking the job, the office server computer died and there was no back-up system. The ministry's fundraising capability was significantly compromised for many months because essential donor records and fundraising program documents were corrupted. In the past, I could always push through and get the job done, even if I had to pull all-nighters. But this was something I couldn't fix. God graciously sent a volunteer who specialized in database recovery to help me, but I couldn't help believing babies were dying because I was incompetent.

At the same time I left my church home of 7 years and all those relationships because I felt God telling me that season was closed and he was going to grow me somewhere else. Without being propped up by those two legs, I couldn't hold back the flood of unhappiness I felt in my marriage.

In my late 30s, head hanging in shame, I sought out a counselor and for the next two years I dedicated myself to allowing God to reveal my brokenness and to wash me as pure as snow (Psalm 51). Many of the principles and concepts I write about in this book I received during this season of my life. I wrestled with looking at marriage vows, theological views regarding biblical grounds for divorce, and the concept of loving well. I'm not for or against divorce, but I do believe God's priority is loving, caring relationships with Him, ourselves, and others. We are called to critique every barrier to loving well and to seek God's wisdom.

I felt very empty emotionally in the marriage. Lewis was a good provider and a good father, but our priorities were different. As with many men, Lewis did not prioritize learning how to meet my God-given emotional and relational needs. It wasn't that he didn't care for me and Ben; his own agenda generally took priority. Many churches acknowledge this issue, but insist this failure is not significant. For me, and for many of my clients, it is.

Recently I spoke with a pastor who explained his denomination believed the only two biblical grounds for divorce were adultery and a non-Christian spouse who wants to leave the marriage. He agreed there were lots of ways spouses could harm each other because of their own brokenness, but he believed more harm would be done if couples separated than staying together. I disagree with such a narrow view of harm. The Bible speaks many times about guarding our heart. If one's heart will be harmed by staying in a relationship of any kind, then I believe God can release us from such commitments. Hearing from God about whether to leave a marriage is always a sober, prayerful decision.

When I could no longer deny my unhappiness, the outpouring of anxiety and depression compromised my ability to function. I desperately wanted to feel better but knew I had no more energy to put into the marriage. I started fights with Lewis and was irritable and unreasonable, hoping he would be the one to quit. Thinking about a second divorce sent me into a downward spiral of punishing self-harm behaviors. I felt so trapped, emotionally starved in the marriage, but wasn't sure God would offer me mercy. I could barely get out of bed in the morning. Lacking motivation and unable to concentrate, taking care of Ben was difficult. Eventually I had to give my notice at work and spent the next three months in a depressed fog.

My counselor kept encouraging me to ask God all my questions rather than assume what He would say. It was really scary to even think of coming before God and telling him what I had done, how I felt, and then wait on His answer. But I kept thinking how I needed to find out what was true because I couldn't keep making such hurtful relationship decisions.

Looking at my amazing, awesome son gave me the strength and courage to persevere. I continuously prayed, *"God, either change my heart or release me from this marriage."* I learned how to sit in God's living room to understand what emotional and relational needs did not get met from key people in my life, setting me up for relationship failure.

Sitting in God's living room is a perspective; it's viewing life circumstances from God's overhead view rather than from a linear viewpoint. My counselor helped me learn how to grieve all the failures; mine and those against me. God convicted me of my own sinful, self-protective responses that hurt others, including Lewis.

During that time I worked at moving towards Lewis, communicating my needs and learning about his comfort zone. From that vulnerable place, I told Lewis what I'd learned about myself and what I needed to be happy and live out my personhood. Although he did not like seeing me so unhappy, Lewis let me know honestly that he was very satisfied with his life. At that point, I believe God spoke to my soul and released me from the marriage. Continuing to expect Lewis to change his life to meet my needs would have been unloving to him. Denying my needs would have been denying who God created me to be. Removing the expectations from our relationship allowed Lewis and me to be much better parents for our son.

While I was working hard on my issues, God began whispering to me about becoming a counselor. After a year, I finally got up the courage to apply to seminary. I knew it would take a miracle for me to be accepted into a graduate school program because although I had three Associate degrees, I did not have a Bachelor's degree. Such a little thing was no problem for God. Within a few weeks, I received my acceptance to Ashland Theological Seminary! After graduation in 2002, I continued to work full time as a law office paralegal and began seeing a few private practice counseling clients out of my house.

Every counselor has to decide what their role is in helping clients. Initially, I thought counselors were supposed to have all the answers to all the problems for all their clients. That was too much responsibility for me! I kept asking God to define my role and he led me to Romans 12:15, *"Rejoice with those who rejoice; mourn with those who mourn."(NIV)* That's it. Create a safe place for people to be vulnerable, share how they are experiencing life, and feel along with them.

Humans are always looking for ways to achieve goals, change circumstances or get rid of feelings. But the Bible seems clear that we are called to walk through life with each other -- not take over God's job by trying to fix people. It's out of the relational caring bond that healing takes place. So although it makes no logical sense that change can occur just by sitting with someone who is grieving, I can testify to the miraculous, transformative healing that comes about when we lift up one another. God's ways are not our ways and His thoughts are not our thoughts. When I looked at my own counseling experience, I saw the growth in my life as my counselor followed this principle. With a mixture of anxiety and excitement, I made a commitment to learn how to be transparent and emotionally vulnerable so that I could show others the way to God's heart.

I distinctly remember one Sunday evening sobbing at the church's altar in 2008, feeling unfulfilled at the law firm and frustrated that I couldn't find a counseling job. God's responded by calling me to establish my own full time private practice. Over the next 10 months I got all my ducks in a row, including wrestling with all my fears about being self-employed with no safety net. I continued to work full time at the law firm as I built up my counseling clients. It was a crazy, busy, awesome, anxiety provoking ride that grew me in many ways. God's timing is so amazing! As I worked 16 hour days and tried to decide when to risk going full time with counseling, the law firm I worked for split up. My boss offered me a part-time position, but God knew I was ready to step out in faith. My calendar has stayed full since that day and I feel like the most blessed person on earth every morning.

I'm passionate about being a counselor and feel honored to walk alongside everyone who comes into my office because I, too, have been on that side of the couch. I know what it's like to be depressed, anxious, scared, neglected, and feel unloved. I learned lots of the same unhealthy self-protective strategies. Because of that, I can go back and walk with clients where they are now, but I can also lay out a vision of what it looks like to be healthy and prosper. I've learned how to be patient in the midst of suffering and talk to God about how He loves and cares for me. I cried, pled, wrestled, prayed, persevered and now can say I am certain that God's plans are always to prosper me. I can joyfully hope into seeing the goodness of the Lord in all circumstances. My heart and my own experience is what I offer as the greatest gift to my clients.

Psalm 23 has been an excellent model. The beginning of the Psalm talks about the shepherd and how he cares for his sheep. David doesn't just give us the job description of a shepherd. He speaks from a place of authority, knowing intimately what the sheep need to be well cared for. There are practical needs like food and water, but also intrinsic needs like emotional wellbeing, a sense of security, and a deep trust in the shepherd who guides them. David shares with us that walking through life in this world involves going through the valley of the shadow of death -- it's not something that can be avoided. As much as the shepherd loves his sheep, David knew there was no earthly path that does not have areas filled with pain and difficulty. This broken world with broken people brings about terribly painful circumstances.

But our Shepherd does not leave his sheep to walk through this world on their own. God reminds us of His presence and His heart for us and we are comforted. He doesn't sit down and have a problem-solving session or encourage us to shut our eyes to avoid the hard places. Instead, God walks beside us, protecting and encouraging us, carrying each one of us on his shoulders when the pain is too great. The Shepherd gives the flock a vision of what they will find on the other side of their trials -- surely goodness, mercy, and love for all the days of our lives as we dwell in the house of the Lord forever. That promise always gives me goose bumps. When we value such a forever treasure over feeling better in the moment, healing has begun to take place. This is why Paul could truthfully look at being in prison as a momentary trouble in light of the unsurpassing joy of knowing God's heart more fully.

What I love most about being a counselor is the ability to "pray without ceasing" all day long. I don't need to be worried about solving problems for clients or giving them a bunch of tools to fix their life. What I do is hang out with them, talk about what they think and feel, and let God direct the conversation. Each day clients will say, "It's funny that you mentioned/asked/said that," and go on to explain how what I just said coincided with something they just heard/read/thought. Coincidence? Nope -- providence! It's amazing to hear from God where to direct the conversation and see hearts open to God and his healing touch.

Since going into this profession, I've learned most counselors focus on either behavioral or cognitive techniques. Cognitive therapists teach clients that if they change their "stinking thinking," their actions will automatically change and they will be "fixed." Behavioral approaches teach clients to "fake it till you make it." Change your behavior first, then your thinking will get on board. Neither of these strategies take feelings into account, which seems very strange to me since pretty much every problem I hear in my office has to do with somebody feeling something! Clinical, medical models of care put people under a microscope. When you're spilling your guts about something shameful, you don't want to be seen as a specimen! As I talk about who I am, my life journey, and my passion for walking with people at their pace, most clients are able to relax and believe I'm a safe person with whom they can share freely. I hope you will have that same experience through my words.

People come to me because their relationships are broken, and I allow that brokenness to play out in the counseling room so we can discuss it and receive God's truth. Looking at beliefs about God, understanding His sovereignty, and asking questions about how He loves us are all an essential part of the healing process.

In order to sit in God's living room and look at events from His perspective, we need to first form a trusting relationship with another human being. Humans hurt humans, so healing generally comes from God through another human. That's what the therapeutic relationship should offer. Part of my role is to allow clients to successfully work through interpersonal conflicts they have with others by learning to be in relationship with me.

The stories my clients tell do truly break my heart. People who are oppressed, poor in spirit, and surrounded by enemies come in with a mustard seed grain of hope that I can help them find God's healing. Teenagers talk about cutting themselves to feel physical pain so they can block out the emotional pain of neglectful parents. Husbands weep in my office over their failure to love their families well because of their own selfishness and immaturity. College students and 20-somethings are terrified of entering the adult world, not sure they have anything of value to offer. Women confess they cannot make an adult relationship work because they've never dealt with their abusive past.

That's why I decided to write this book, to share with the world what I've learned as a counselor about how to love and care for God, ourselves, and others. It's a very different process, but one I believe is based on godly principles and lived out by Jesus and the disciples. What I want for my clients and you, my dear readers, is to be rooted and established in God's heart of love so that together, we can all grasp how wide and long and high and deep is the love of Christ. (Ephesians 3:17-19 NIV) Such amazing love surpasses cognitive knowledge, but fills our soul to the brim with the fullness of God.

I once longed to be grounded in consistency and purpose instead of living in turmoil and despair. Today, I live in that place. It was through my own valley of the shadow of death journey that God planted His truths in my soul. Truth has brought stability and security, anchoring me through difficult times, allowing me to embrace Christ's love through it all. The Roadmap to Freedom comes out of my own struggles and is based on God's word. I'm excited to walk along as you boldly undertake this transformative journey. I ask God to bless you with strength, courage, healing, and hope.

REFLECTION QUESTIONS

1. Did you have hopes and dreams as a child that were dismissed, minimized, or given up on?
2. Does it feel like you set yourself aside or gave up on believing in yourself?
3. How thick is your protective armor?
4. Does your armor truly protect you from others and from your own feelings?
5. What is the cost to your relationships and quality of life to maintain your armor?
6. How much do fear, shame, and guilt impact your life?
7. Do you know how to grieve well?
8. What beliefs do you have/been given about the role of emotions?
9. What difficult journeys have you faced and what blessings have you found in the process?
10. Have you given up hope of living a joyful, prospering life

What's Love Got to Do With It?

$\mathbf{D}$id you know there are 1,189 songs with "Love" in the title written from the 1950s to present? There are tons of songs, books, and movies focusing on all aspects of love. Seems like we all have a hard time figuring out how to love God, our spouse, our children, ourselves, and even our neighbor well. John 13:34 gives us the commandment to love one another -- yet this is impossible to do in our own strength. Since we disconnected from the source of love when Adam & Eve left the Garden, humankind has been scrambling to figure out how to love well based on our own understanding. This is where viewpoint is important, because the answer is found in the principles of relationship, not created through a series of behaviors or found in a roller coaster of feelings.

Models of Relationship

What is love? Most people answer this question by talking about specific feelings and behaviors. Very few of us can articulate the type of relationship model we want to live out. Most folks don't realize they are living out the same unhealthy model in all their relationships, which explains why things don't work out over and over again. In my office, I draw three different models of relationships and ask clients which one they saw growing up and which one they currently living out. I categorize relationship models into three main areas: Narcissistic, Negotiation, and Relational.

Narcissistic Model

One person lives within the comfort zone of the other

Narcissistic relationships center on the comfort zone of one person. Conversation topics, activities, TV shows, etc. are all controlled by one person. If you try to include the dominant person in something they have no interest in, they'll walk away, change the subject, or make fun of you. All these behaviors are designed to get the other person to shut up and leave them alone. The Narcissistic relationship looks like the old *All In The Family* sitcom. Archie Bunker sat in his chair in the living room and made himself the center of the household. He lived completely in his comfort zone, demanding everyone come to him. His wife, Edith, catered to his wishes and when she hesitantly asked Archie to meet one of her needs, he became a bully, intimidating her to the point where she apologized for bringing it up. The dominant person learns what words and actions will get them what they want. Sometimes that's getting someone to back off and stop asking them for something. Other times, the dominate person wants something and figures out how to badger, intimidate or manipulate others to get it. The dominant person can manifest as 1) a mean bully, 2) someone who chooses isolation, or 3) a victim/emotional black hole.

For every narcissist, you will often find a "loving" co-dependent partner, one who doesn't know the difference between being loved as a person and used as a resource. The only role for the co-dependent in this model is to give up their own personhood and live completely within the dominant person's circle. I define personhood as permission to own one's thoughts, emotions, opinions, and actions. When personhood is denied or locked away, we live a submissive, robotic existence. Our personhood encapsulates the most interesting and unique qualities God created in us.

Although my example is dated, unfortunately, there are plenty of present day Archies and Ediths in every sector of life, especially in abusive situations. Did you watch *The Amazing Race Season 6*? Jonathan became infamous for his treatment of wife Victoria. He was verbally abusive, belittling, and controlling. In Berlin, he intentionally pushed her down, then berated her for crying. For someone to successfully walk away from such an abusive relationship, they need to understand and grieve the lie they are not capable of anything more meaningful.

Omarosa, on the first season of *The Apprentice* and *American Idol's* Simon Cowell may be examples of the self-contained, condescending Narcissistic model type. They very clearly give the message that everyone else is beneath them and no one else's opinion matters.

The hardest dominant type to pinpoint is the emotionally needy black hole person. A good example is the Michael Scott character on *The Office*. I enjoy watching that show and have a soft spot for Michael and his dramatic histrionics. But Michael's self-serving, victim mentality would be exhausting to live with day in and day out. Clients of both genders complain how their relationship centers on their spouse's emotional needs. The dominant spouse needs constant affirmation, looking to the co-dependent for approval, withholding affection or even finances if the client doesn't give them enough attention. In this relationship model, only one person's opinions, thoughts, feelings, and needs count.

Negotiation Model

The Negotiation relationship model focuses on business-type transactional exchanges to meet needs. Each person is a separate, distinct entity, like two separate planets. Sometimes they move toward each other to accomplish tasks or enjoy times together. When the task or event ends, each person retreats inside their own orbit, solely responsible for their own wellbeing.

Bargaining is the currency of this relationship in *"do this for me and I'll let you do that for you"* type interactions. It's a step up from the Narcissistic model because the two people are able to move out of their comfort zones towards the other. However, the level of willingness to sacrifice is usually measured by what someone gets.

People often settle for this model when the person they care about cannot or chooses not to work towards living out the Relational model. The cost of this strategy is learning how to push down the longing for more. In my years of experience, guys usually try to figure out what is the least amount of work or time they need to put in to appease their gal and stop her nagging. Knowing this, the gal generally gets the message that she is "too needy." Not wanting to be seen "as a burden," the gal only asks for the bare minimum from her guy, trying to protect herself against disappointment. Truth is, we gals ARE disappointed and denying it only causes bitterness to grow. We hate ourselves for wanting more and feel helpless at seeing how we take out our resentment on others. Instead, God wants to empower us gals to love our guy well by holding the maturity bar high. Guys, too, can feel helpless to live up to their gal's expectations.

I was recently at a restaurant and struck up a conversation with three buddies in their 30s who were in town for a reunion with college friends. After reading a text, one of the men excused himself and went outside to make a phone call. On his return, he said his wife had overdrawn their account by $7,000 on a furniture spending spree. He reported she justified the purchase by angrily pointing out he took a vacation without her. The husband began rehearsing the rebuttal speech he was going to deliver when he got home. The Negotiation style of relationship is a human-created strategy, usually ending in a cold, distant stalemate, lingering disappointment, or a nagging, bitter, resentful undercurrent.

Relational Model

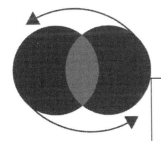

Each person pursues the other in the areas where their lives do not directly overlap

The Relational approach is based on interdependence on God and each other and has a "one another" focus. We move toward each other, enjoying the direct overlap of our lives, and proactively pursuing each other in the indirect areas. When our partner can't directly experience an area of life with us or meet a need, they can move towards us by listening, encouraging, inspiring, and comforting.

Allowing God to heal our own baggage and mature us individually has a direct impact on our relationships and our capability to support the other person's growth. "One anotherness" is about heart attitude; each person intentionally turning their heart toward the other. It's like the look between a long time married couple when they're remembering an inside joke or something in the present that reminds them of a shared past experience. Being present and engaged in each other's life allows you to learn more about each other and use that information to strengthen your connection. Needs are seen as opportunities to show love to each other.

My son Ben has had a fascination with sports cards and memorabilia since he was little. I'd buy him a pack of cards and we would look at the players together, talking about who we each liked and for what reason. My criteria involved a big smile or pretty blue eyes while Ben appreciated all the stats and records. I didn't have a clue as to why one brand of cards had a higher monetary value than another or why one particular player's card was a rare find. What I did know was that Ben loved sharing his knowledge and passion for cards with me. Moving toward him in this area allowed the light of his joy and excitement to brighten my day.

We are meant to live life in the presence of one another. That can look many ways, but it's determined by the intent of our heart to be known intimately. As a human being, Jesus surrounded himself with people who lived with him every day. He could have done it differently, kept himself separate and apart from people until it was time for his sacrifice on the cross. But he didn't. Instead, Jesus chose to walk alongside humankind, giving everyone the opportunity to interact and experience him personally. When we can feel out someone's heart and character, it allows us to forge a relational bond. I believe everyone who had an encounter with Jesus came away knowing he saw straight through to their heart.

My guess is some people hated being exposed. For most, however, it gave them the courage to look at their own strengths and weaknesses. I can honestly say I hate it when my family or friends point something unknown out to me. But if I've got lipstick on my teeth or I'm about to rear-end the car in front of me, I want to know about it! And if I'm not loving them well, I want them to have the confidence to bring it to my attention. Choosing to withstand that momentary rush of defensiveness and opting for a heart-to-heart connection is well worth the sacrifice.

Barriers to Living the Relational Model

One of the hardest relational skills is knowing where to draw the line in stepping into someone's life. The easiest answer is to live out of a rulebook, demanding everyone follow the same set of expectations. Connecting to God's heart, however, provides the relational wisdom to show each person love in the way they were designed to need it most. As human beings, we make decisions in life revolving around avoiding hurt and pain, especially related to those we love. But the Bible shows a different model. Jesus so loved us, he was willing to undergo physical and emotional pain to show us the extent of his love. It's never easy to see someone we care about hurt, but pain is often a necessary catalyst for change and growth.

Romans 8:28 challenges us to grow in our ability to trust in God's heart and motives when we, in our limited capacity for understanding, do not see love in action on the surface. My son did not always understand why I didn't fulfill his every request, sometimes feeling disappointed and misunderstood. But as our relationship grew, Ben came to trust in my motives because he rested securely in my love for him.

I love that there's no "one size fits all" answer with God. I don't believe we are instructed to turn the other cheek for everyone nor are we to call everyone a "white washed tomb" as Jesus did to the Pharisees. When I run to God and ask how to love well, sometimes He tells me to say or do something immediately. Other times I'm instructed to just listen and validate feelings. In some circumstances, God tells me it's best for us both if I love people from a distance in a prayerful way. A Relational approach to life involves learning how to receive clarity from God about how we best support other people's learning curve. Many times this looks like stepping back and allowing our loved ones to experience hurt and pain as a result of their own immature decisions and rigid beliefs so they will seek God.

Jesus' interaction with the rich young ruler in Luke 18 is a good example of this principle. This ruler had worked hard to follow all the commandments since he was a young boy. The account leads us to believe he was serious about his relationship with God. He had put time, effort, and energy into following the guidelines set out by the religious establishment. But even after being a model pupil, this ruler recognized the religious system could not assure him of God's acceptance.

The ruler heard about a new teacher named Jesus and sought him out to ask him the burning question of how to achieve eternal life. I find Jesus' response fascinating. The first thing he did was to challenge the ruler on the issue of Jesus' credentials. When people are not ready to hear God's answer to their question, they go shopping. Hearing something they don't like from one source, people often rationalize and discount the source, then go searching for another opinion. I wonder how many "good teachers" this ruler had approached with this question. Jesus immediately established the fact that only God alone is the "good teacher" and if we ask God a question, we need to be open to hearing and receiving His truthful answers.

Jesus led the ruler to the heart of the matter by exposing his flawed life strategy. The ruler had been taught to keep every single commandment, assuring him he would receive God's approval. Jesus points out that knowing information and blindly following rules never results in knowing God or others intimately. God's strategy for our life is based on inner heart attitude rather than outward obedience. Jesus told the ruler to sell everything he had, give it to the poor, then leave home and come travel with him as a disciple. Luke 18:23 says the ruler sadly turned away. Unlike following a straight-forward set of commandments, Jesus' words necessitates wrestling with heartfelt sacrifice as well as external cost.

Humankind has developed a hierarchy that relies on wealth, rules, status, etc. to bestow worth and value. God tells us,

> The Lord does not look at the things man looks at. Man looks at the outward appearance, but the Lord looks at the heart. (I Samuel 16:7 NIV)

We set up rules and systems that make it possible for people to build their own Tower of Babel and reach up to God. But we are fooling ourselves because God always talks about heart attitude, intent, motivation, and character -- and those things can never be achieved by simply obeying commandments.

The rich young ruler was saddened that the cost of being with God meant bankrupting himself financially in the present life. The life strategy he was taught caused him to ask Jesus the wrong question.

Rather than seeking to know what hoops he needed to jump through to get the prize, he should have been asking how to draw closer to God's heart. Viewing the world from God's heart changes our perspective on everything.

I want to believe this ruler eventually sold all he had and went to follow Jesus. I hope this encounter with Jesus caused the ruler to come to the Apostle Peter's belief that only Jesus has the words of life. Transformation of our humanistic life strategy brings us into the presence of the Almighty God, a gift that trumps all earthly treasures. But maybe all he could see was what he would give up and he learned how to shut off his disappointment so he could continue living by the rules.

I do acknowledge the rich young ruler was apparently living a very good lifestyle, making it easier to focus on the positive. That's not the case for most of the people coming into my office. They tell me stories of hurt and heartache that has or is presently happening to them or to people they love. Everyone on this planet hopes for a quick solution that will stop pain and head them toward happiness. No matter which position you are in, the Bible is clear that the price of healing is truthfully seeking out all the self-protective ways that separate us from the love of God.

John 8:32 promises that God's truth will set us free when we commit to a lifestyle of asking hard questions and sitting in painful feelings. Truth is not a scientific conclusion arrived at by examination of data. It cannot be separated from the person of God.

> Truth has a name [Jesus]...Everything is about him. And freedom is a process that happens inside a relationship with him. (Young, p. 95)

I picture this freedom as waking up to Christmas morning every day. I'm excited to walk through the day, receiving new revelations of who I am as I view myself through relationship with Jesus. I look forward to learning how I can better live the abundant life today, all the while giving thanks to God for my unique qualities and gifts.

Jesus was at the pool of Bethesda one day and started up a conversation with a man who talked about being crippled for 38 years. He explained to Jesus that every so often, an angel would stir the pool and the first person to get into the water was healed. Jesus asked the man a very interesting question. *"Do you want to be healed?" (John 5:6 NIV)*

Now why would Jesus ask that question? Obviously the man wanted to be healed, he had just told Jesus all about his physical ailments and how he spent his entire day waiting at the pool. It seems like a very illogical question on its surface, but there were lots of reasons why it was critical Jesus ask that question of that man -- and why God asks it of each one of us.

> *Sir, the invalid replied, I have no one to help me into the pool when the water is stirred. While I am trying to get in, someone else goes down ahead of me. (John 5:7 NIV)*

The man's response shows hope in his healing had dwindled down to almost nothing. He had no one who cared enough to be by his side to help him. We can often feel like the victim of a loveless world and get caught up in hating our weaknesses. At those times we need Jesus to ask this obvious question designed to challenge our ingrained monologue of hopelessness. This question shed light on the invalid's despairing heart and gave him the opportunity to anchor to truth. Hope for healing and happiness must come out of our understanding of God's heart for our full transformation. Changes in circumstances are temporary. Hope in God's heart for us is always assured. Holding tight to this truth will change us for eternity.

Another barrier to grasping the power of relationship is our current culture of independence and separateness. We receive praise for pulling up our own bootstraps, paying our way through college, relying only on ourselves and not being a burden on others.

What does God say about this way of life? Jesus told a parable about a shepherd leaving his 99 sheep to go out and bring the lost one back to the fold. This is a great example of how living the Relational model brings care, comfort, and protection into our life. There is amazing strength in living an interrelated life. People who've been involved in terrible circumstances testify what got them through were memories of their loved ones. Passengers on United Airlines Flight 93 on September 11, 2001 used their love of family and country to gain the strength and courage necessary to overcome the hijackers. Husbands have taken bullets for their wives and mothers have faced wild animals to save their children. Strangers stop on the side of the road to help a person in trouble. When we look at the world through "one another" eyes, we can see God in the words and deeds of those around us.

Jesus so desired a relationship with us that he set aside the fullness of his union with the trinity to wholly embrace humanness. Even in his limited capacity, Jesus had enough relational currency to love well. Reading the gospel accounts, we see the power of being in a relationship with Jesus. In the short time he was here on earth, his presence brought about healing, freedom from oppression, and redemption of personhood. Those things did not happen because Jesus was God. They happened because he allowed himself to be a dependent, limited human being. Jesus relied on his relationship to ask God the Father to care for others well. When we get a better understanding of being created in the image of God, we'll be excited about harnessing the power of relationship.

Learning to Love Ourselves First

Have you ever looked into a snow globe and wished you could live in such an idyllic setting? Before we can do relationship with others well, we need to revel in how God loves us. That means learning how to close out the world and sit inside God's heart. Ask God to shut out everything clamoring for your attention and develop a special, unique place in your soul where the two of you can communicate. I do this by reading Psalms to hear David talk about God's loving kindness and feeling Moses' frustration with stiff-necked Israelites. Be inspired by Peter's zealousness and go on an emotional roller coaster with John to share Jesus' last days. Listen to music that stirs your heart. Sad, mad, joyful -- pour out all your feelings in the safety of the snow globe and God will share Himself with you. What we gain is a different way to view ourselves and others through God's eyes.

A good example of this is when Jesus was invited to have dinner with a Pharisee named Simon. A woman anointed Jesus' feet with her tears and wiped them dry with her hair, kissing his feet and pouring perfume on them. From the Pharisee's viewpoint, she was a known sinner and he would never have allowed such an unclean person to touch him. Jesus told a parable to help Simon see what the woman already knew about forgiveness and mercy. God's viewpoint always starts with seeing how much He cares for us. Despite our weaknesses, it's His loving kindness that leads us to repentance and new life. Outside the snow globe, humankind sets up artificial standards and judges whether people measure up. When we view the world through relationship with God, there is love, grace, mercy, compassion, and acceptance.

Once we choose this Relational model, there's a learning curve to understand how to live it out every day. First, learn how to be vulnerable, sharing with safe people your life experiences and receiving care and encouragement in return. Talking about your day always involves sharing and venting feelings. That process uncovers beliefs about how the world should work, what we think God feels about us, what we deserve, etc.

Most of the beliefs we hold came from a fallen world system rather than from God. All of us have beliefs about what it looks like to be a good Christian, good spouse, good parent, etc. When we fall short of the standard we've adopted, we generally use self-punishing, punitive tactics to get ourselves back on the straight and narrow path to perfection. It's those beliefs and tactics that need to be identified and critiqued. The woman who anointed Jesus' feet lived out the belief that God had completely forgiven her and wanted her to walk in freedom. The Relational model assures us of God's love for us unconditionally; the human Outcome-based model instills doubt and fear.

Most of us ask the wrong questions in life because they come out of fear. We question whether we're doing the wrong thing, what other people will think of us, and list all the "what if" catastrophic things that could happen.

Fear is a powerful tool of the enemy because it causes us to focus solely on ourselves. When we're locked in fear, our entire focus is on getting relief and feeling better. Anxiety and panic throw us into survival mode where we view the world through a narrow, black and white grid making us feel isolated, alone, abandoned, weak, incompetent, etc. Questions such as *How does God feel about me when I mess up?* and *How did I become broken?* lead us to a place where we're able to see God and ourselves clearly.

In Psalm 51, David prays that he will cultivate a contrite spirit so he can be sensitive to God. Although God's answers to these questions can bring us sadness and disappointment, accepting the truth brings freedom and strength rather than fear.

God has given us unique ways of looking at the world. The process of growth and change will look differently for each one of us. We have four gospels because each author's experience of the same events was significant. Each account provides insight into the writer and their relationship with Jesus. Their differing perspectives reached a different set of people, drawing them into relationship with God.

Unfortunately, there often isn't a lot of tolerance in the Christian community for messy, out-of-the-box growth processes. Most pastors and leaders are much more comfortable when everyone follows the same guidelines as that strategy allows them to easily judge progress. The Bible shows Jesus supported everyone in their own individual growth plan, from Zacchaeus to the Roman Centurion to lovable Peter. Jesus' example gives me permission to work out my own salvation (Galatians).

Applying the Relational Model

I love watching the Hallmark channel! Yes, I know the movies are often superficial and cheesy, but that's why I watch them. Real life and real relationships have a lot of pain and frustration. Being able to watch a movie knowing I will cry in the middle and sigh over the happy-ever-after ending gives me a sense of comfort and predictability. My son Ben will come into the room, watch me for a few minutes, then point at me saying, "There it is, you're making that sappy face." I tell him there's nothing wrong with a little sappiness in this world!

The general storyline in Hallmark movies goes like this: 1) two people start a new relationship; 2) difficult situation causes re-evaluation of their relationship and what they believe about the other person; 3) trusted person tells them to look at their own issues; 4) conviction leads them to give grace and forgiveness to the other person; and 5) they re-establish their relationship in a deeper, truer way. Ahhhh, don't we all wish it actually worked that way in our lives?

Truthfully, I don't think this plot is entirely wrong. What I do take issue with is how it gives folks the mistaken idea they should be able to work through their own problems and get to the happy-ever-after part in 1:59 or less. Many clients over the years have been discouraged when longstanding relational problems don't change after a few heart-felt conversations.

Jesus had lots of conversations with his disciples that caused them to look at themselves. Look at James and John who sent their mother to Jesus on his way to Jerusalem to ask if her sons could sit at the head table in heaven after he died. Jesus spoke to the disciples about their heart attitudes and invited them into the snow globe to experience a loving, sacrificial lifestyle. We can see from their writings that James and John matured, using Jesus' words as an invitation to let go of the world's definition of authority-based leadership and embrace a godly relational one.

Many people dismiss the idea of working through problems in a way that keeps the relationships intact as a fairy tale. Maybe when you've told people how they've hurt or disappointed you, things got worse and your words were met with anger and defensiveness. Maybe the other person walked away and the relationship was ruined. That's where it's helpful to understand which relationship model you are using. When you keep living out the same unhealthy cycle, it's hard to believe there's a healthy way to do relationship this side of heaven. I've had the privilege of learning how to work through issues within an important relationship.

My counseling colleague, Mark, and I have been friends for many years. Our sons Ben and Brian were on a couple of the same high school summer baseball teams. One day I mentioned going back to school for a counseling degree. Mark shared he'd graduated from Ashland Theological Seminary, saw clients in private practice, and offered to answer any questions. That was the beginning of many conversations about grad school, what it took to be a good counselor, how to be your own boss, etc. Mark encouraged me to apply to Ashland, saying he honestly believed I would make a good counselor. He saw qualities in me that I seriously doubted in myself. However, his words, along with input from other important people in my life, led me to take a chance and apply.

I graduated in 2002 and entered into private practice, part-time at first and eventually I made it my full time job. Mark and I kept in touch and I appreciated his wisdom and insights, both on how to be good for the client and how to run a successful business. Several years later Mark contacted me and suggested we lease an office suite together. Remaining individual entities, it helped us financially to share office expenses and provide professional support. He brought along another counselor, Kathy, and we've become a tight knit group.

All three of us have the same underlying belief that God created us to learn how to give and receive love well. We live that out in our own lives and it forms the foundation of our counseling. It's been interesting to see the individual differences between us. Kathy is richly emotional and her heart for others is evident as she thanks me profusely for making a pot of coffee or getting her computer to connect to the Internet. She's unpretentiously chic with her short, dark hair and petite frame. I love how she creatively decorated the waiting room in a way that makes our clients feel comfortable and safe. Her office is brimming over with eclectic furniture, cherished mementos, and a delicate femininity that perfectly captures her personality.

In contrast, Mark's office is utilitarian. He has an expansive corner office with floor to ceiling windows on two sides and barely anything in the room! His minimalistic style creates a peaceful sanctuary in the midst of a messy world. Most days he reminds me of the absent-minded professor. He misplaces just about everything he touches. In his 50s, Mark's gray hair always needs cutting and the holes in his jeans are not intentional fashion statements! Mark can often be found talking to himself while walking in and out of the building, trying to remember what he's forgotten. When he stops and focuses on you, however, his honesty, integrity, and love for people and God is apparent. Mark's been counseling folks for almost 25 years and his ability to discern the root of issues has been life changing for many. We've had great conversations about how men grow and mature differently from women and the difficulties of men to live out their roles as husbands and fathers.

Clients say my office is cozy and inviting like me. Standing 5' tall, my most memorable features are my blue eyes and short hair that leans toward auburn or blonde, depending on my mood the last time I visited my hairdresser! As you walk in, my desk is on the left with my diplomas above it and a bookcase on the right with photos of my trip to Israel and Pittsburgh Steeler memorabilia. I like the balance I've achieved between the intimate conversation area and my desk and files. My chair and client couch are next to the large window. I hung a beautiful print on the wall above the couch that has lots of yellow sunflowers planted under a bright blue sky.

Kathy, Mark, and I also have very different skill sets which, when used for the benefit of the group, allows us to have the complete package. What I hate to do, Mark is comfortable with. What stresses Kathy out, is no big deal to me. Mark takes care of the physical office needs, deals with the lease and the landlord, does the heavy lifting, confronts difficult people, makes lots of dumb jokes, and shows us silly animal YouTube videos. Kathy enjoys creating an inviting office atmosphere for the clients and staff. She adds all the little thoughtful, pretty, creative touches the rest of us don't usually put thought and time into doing. I'm very comfortable wearing the office manager hat which includes dealing with technology, supplies, refilling the paper in the copy machine and fax, reminding people of important deadlines, and dealing with all kinds of paperwork.

About a year ago, Mark rented out an extra office in our suite to a psychiatrist who works with the substance abuse population. I began noticing his clients would sometimes wander around the office, going behind the receptionist's desk and even into offices. Feeling very uncomfortable, I asked Mark to talk to the doctor. He did so, but nothing changed. One evening I came out to the receptionist's desk and two of our laptops had been stolen. When I reported it to Mark, he appeared to shrug it off, saying things like that happened and he guessed we'd just have to buy new computers. That made me even angrier than the theft itself. I felt like Mark was dismissing my feelings and disregarding my unspoken internal expectation that it was his duty to keep me safe.

The next day Mark checked in to see how I was feeling and I told him I needed some time to process. Over the next couple of days I wrestled with my desire to run away vs. seeing this as an opportunity to grow relationally. As I prayed, I realized the thing I was most fearful about was our relationship.

I was afraid if I talked to Mark about my hurt feelings, he would behave in the same hurtful ways many other people had done in the past. But if I didn't have that conversation, I would respond out of my old unhealthy pattern to detach and run away. The disappointment in losing that relationship would be a lifelong regret.

During my time on the other side of the couch, I learned how to challenge that self-protective way of doing life. My therapist taught me to prioritize moving towards safe people, especially when they hurt me. God challenged me to risk being vulnerable with Mark, promising to be with me no matter the outcome.

I asked Mark if we could talk about the incident and he gladly agreed. Mark did a great job making it safe for me to tell him I was disappointed in him. I was incredibly anxious. My words tumbled out without making a lot of rational sense, just a jumbled mess of feelings.

Mark validated my emotions, but also correctly pointed out that my level of fear and anger about the incident was disproportionate to the circumstances. That usually means past emotional baggage is triggered by present events. I owned my issues, understanding I needed to separate out past from present. When Mark asked what I needed from him to feel safe in the office, I was able to see his heart and it strengthened our relationship.

That conversation was light years away from ones I've had with other people throughout my life. Most of the time, people got defensive and deflected anything I said about their behaviors, pushing it back on me. Mark respected my feelings and concerns, but cared enough to share truth.

Because of the caring way Mark received me, I was able to hear his suggestions and I spent time reflecting on the root of my feelings. The incident brought up feelings of being put in danger and of feeling personally violated. A child part of me looked at Mark as a father figure and felt that he should have protected me from this pain. The teenage part felt like he initially dismissed my feelings, telling me I had no value or worth. As these incorrect messages came to light, I was able to separate out past hurt and pain from the present circumstances and Mark's true character.

We talked about the pros and cons of allowing the doctor and his patients to remain. Mark assured me that if I was unable to feel safe in the office, he would ask the psychiatrist to leave the suite. I was on high anxiety status the days the doctor was in the office, but eventually I regained my sense of wellbeing. It did help to see Mark police the waiting room and I learned to speak up when patients were overly loud or intrusive.

To me, this account would make a great Hallmark movie. It shows the authentic process of wrestling through your own individual issues for the sake of maintaining important relationships. Oh, and I would really like Sandra Bullock to play my part. I think she'd look great as a redhead!

REFLECTION QUESTIONS

1. Which model of relationship do you primarily live out?
2. What keeps you engaged in Narcissistic or Negotiation relationships?
3. In what ways would you need to grow and heal in order to live a Relational lifestyle?
4. How do you react when God or another person points out your weaknesses?
5. What resentments do you hold against God and others?
6. In what ways do you have a self-protective, flawed life strategy?
7. What barriers keep you from living a truthful life?
8. How well do you love yourself and others?
9. How do you think God feels about you, especially when you mess up?
10. Do you want to FEEL better or BE better?

CHAPTER 3

How Did It Go Wrong?

Looking through a keyhole, you base your impression of a room on a tiny sliver of information. If you try to analyze your weaknesses through the lens of self-condemnation, you'll completely miss the bigger context. Paul gives us a perfect example of this process in Romans 7. He was very frustrated with seeing his own weaknesses, so in Romans 8 he goes back to the basics to get understanding and clarity. Starting on the Roadmap to Freedom begins with looking at the big picture of life. This viewpoint provides context, helping you to understand why life's not working out the way you hoped.

Why Are We Here?

I believe this is the most important question we can ask as human beings. We're told in Genesis 5:1 that God created us in His image, but why? I've been in church and among the Christian community all my life. Between my own experiences and accounts from my clients, I hear the same standard responses. In 2 Timothy, Paul challenges us to critique our beliefs so we can defend our faith. It's vitally important for each person to wrestle with this foundational question. The belief we adopt provides the interpretive glasses through which we view everything in life. To that end, I'm offering you an opportunity to try on a few of these "glasses" below and experience what life looks and feels like from each standard response perspective.

Belief 1: We are created to preach the Gospel to the world.

Lifestyle: Focused on looking for opportunities to directly evangelize everyone around you at all times.

Cost: Living a joyful life in the present is sacrificed to focus on religious duty making life feel burdensome.

Belief 2: We are created to give all of ourselves to care for and minister to others.

Lifestyle: Put others first, sacrifice your own needs to give to others without expectation of reward or recognition.

Cost: Without a balance between loving others and loving ourselves, we can become bitter and resentful, an easy target to be used and manipulated by others.

Belief 3: We owe God our entire life because he sacrificed himself for our sinfulness and disobedience.

Lifestyle: Constant reminders of being fundamentally broken without worth or value. The debt I owe to God is greater than I can ever repay.

Cost: Life of self-condemnation, discouragement, overcompensating for inadequacies, and living an independent life unable to receive from God and others.

Belief 4: We must live a disciplined life to become Christ-like.

Lifestyle: Everything is run through a very narrow black and white grid of what is/is not godly.

> *Cost:* Denial of our own personhood to follow someone else's standard of godliness.

While I agree with the principles of sharing God with others, caring for those around us, acknowledging our weaknesses, and following Christ's model on earth, I don't believe any one of these responses answers the question. God did not primarily create us to be his lackeys; He certainly has all the resources he needs to impact our world. Nor did God create us to aspire to be his perfect clones or robots. Look at all the varieties of animals and plants God created simply for enjoyment. The Pauline epistles talk about God intentionally giving us unique gifts and talents.

I believe it's very clear we were joyfully created for God to pour out His love on us and to teach us how to love and be loved well. That's it. Everything we think, do, and feel in life becomes abundantly clear when we interpret it through that truth. Paul excitedly shares this good news in Romans 8:14-16 NIV:

> *Because those who are led by the Spirit of God are sons of God. For you did not receive a spirit that makes you a slave again to fear, but you received the spirit of sonship. And by him we cry, 'Abba, Father.' The Spirit himself testifies with our spirit that we are God's children.*

Truth is, we are God's children and He loves us completely and wants us to live our life out of that unshakeable foundation. How different would your life look and feel if you never questioned God's heart of love for you? Such a life begins with examining your belief about why God created humankind. The beliefs I listed above will help us live the life God gives us, but they're not meant to become a substitute for relationship.

Rather than spending the majority of our time focusing on doing Christian things well, God wants us to seek his input on what barriers keep us from giving and receiving love. Once you have the correct viewpoint of sonship, Mark 12:30-31 NIV becomes the roadmap for life.

> *Love the Lord your God with all your heart and with all your soul and with all your mind and with all your strength. The second is this, Love your neighbor as yourself. There is no commandment greater than these.*

In the Beginning

If the foundation of our life is based on loving well, then how did we get so off track? It started in the Garden of Eden. Relationships on earth began the moment God breathed life into Adam. Dysfunctional relationships began the moment Adam and Eve believed the serpent's lies about God's character and intent.

Genesis tells us that in the beginning, Adam walked with God every day. God already knew every detail of his creation, yet chose to experience Adam in this personal, intimate, relational way. Adam shared his thoughts and feelings with God as he went about his day. I believe Adam talked to God about his loneliness and need to spend time with another human being. This was not a surprise to God, for part of being made in the image of God is the foundational need for community. But I believe God waited for Adam to recognize and share this core longing before he created Eve. Adam's joyful response shows his gratefulness for God meeting such a deep need.

God continued to interact with both Adam and Eve in a personal, intimate way; walking and talking with them, delighting in their enjoyment of all He had created specifically for them. That relational connection allowed them to know and believe in the righteousness of God's character. Because of that belief, they were able to trust that God's heart was always loving towards them. Then entered doubt.

Most likely, the serpent had been whispering to Adam and Eve for a long while. Every time they walked past the forbidden tree, the serpent probably whispered doubts about God's motivation and questioned his trustworthiness.

> Did God really want their best? Why did he deny them something that was good to their eyes and not let them make their own choice? What exactly was God's motive in creating them and giving them such a temptation?

Every human being has these big picture questions, whether whispered deep down or shouted with a fist raised to the sky. Human beings question God's motives. When circumstances do not line up with what we believe we deserve or what we've been taught God should allow, we blame God. Sometimes we tell God he's unfair. Other times we're so disappointed, we distance ourselves from him.

The serpent tempted Adam and Eve with the ability to take full control of their own decision-making. Why risk someone else, even God, not having my best interests at heart? I suspect each one of us would have made the same decision to have autonomy and ultimate control over our own life. I know at one time I would have made that decision.

Take a minute right now to check deep down at the very bottom of your soul. Do you truly believe God loves you and is actively caring for you every minute of every day through every circumstance? Most of you will be courageous enough to admit no, you don't completely believe.

So what do you do now? Be truthful and talk to God and safe other people about your doubts. Sweeping the worries under the rug and doing a bunch of good works only give the doubts more credibility and the enemy starts whispering even louder. When we believe God loves and cares for us completely, we can bring all our anxieties to him, even worries about God himself. Without that viewpoint, we're open to the enemy's lies about God's heart for us. Oftentimes we have a lot of fear surrounding what God thinks and feels about us. Learning how to have these conversations with one another helps us to boldly go before God. I spend a lot of time in my office making it safe for clients to admit they have questions about God.

Asking the Hard Questions

Many people, churches, and even countries are intimidated by someone raising hard questions and advocating boldness. For some, questioning any level of authority is seen as rebelliousness. I see it as an opportunity to honorably wrestle with important relational beliefs. In the Old Testament, Jacob wrestled all night with the Angel of God, declaring he would not let go until God blessed him. The angel could've easily overpowered Jacob at any time. Through his persever-ance, Jacob was strengthened and grew in his understanding of him-self and God. Jacob came away from that encounter with an experiential knowledge of God's heart and character that he couldn't have learned any other way.

Struggling with complicated topics like making hard decisions, hurt and heartache, "why" questions, etc. produces a strength of char-acter, will, and determination which propel us to live the abundant life in the midst of a broken world. The caterpillar spins a cocoon when it's time to transform into a butterfly. Even when the physical change has taken place, it must struggle to break open the cocoon. The wings need strengthened to be able to fly and live a new life as a butterfly. Without that struggle, it dies without ever fully living. So, too, each of us must individually wrestle with our questions and doubts to live in the freedom truth brings.

I look at how governments in countries such as China prioritize compliancy over individuality. They seek out and ruthlessly silence those who question government mandates. Any spark of originality threatens a structured system where the only thing that matters is maintaining absolute authority and control. Sadly, there are many examples of churches and religious communities who also use violence or other means of manipulative control to make sure parishioners do not ask questions. Threats of violence or excommunication keep citizens and congregations powerless.

God does not take offense to questions and doubts when they lead us to His throne. Sinfulness did not occur because Adam and Eve questioned God's heart. It came about when, despite having all the factual and experiential truth, they chose self-protection. Rather than using their questions to pursue a better understanding of God, Adam and Eve settled for relying on their limited capacity for understanding and judged God's heart. Satan's goal is always to encourage us to doubt God's motives and, therefore, His character.

Relational Impact of Adam & Eve's Fall

At the moment when Adam and Eve acted upon their conclusion and chose control over relationship, their eyes were opened and the pair realized they were naked. I don't think this passage was talking about their physical eyes. Instead, this talks about looking at themselves and each other through relational eyes. In that instant, realizing they were cut off from the source of love, all the responsibility for loving well rested solely on each individual. What an unimaginable heavy burden that realization must have been. How, in the name of all that is holy, were they supposed to know themselves, each other, and God so intimately well that they could do relationship perfectly?

I imagine panic set in pretty quickly, especially as they heard God calling for them in the Garden. This was the first relational test on their own and how did they handle it? They hid, lied about it, and then pointed fingers at each other. The ability to be humble, sacrificial, and truthful was decimated when the connection to God was severed.

How utterly tragic for them and for all of humankind. The relational consequences experienced by the generations following Adam and Eve's removal from the garden have been devastating.

Prior to banishment, the relationship between husband, wife, and God was an unending flow of care and love between and among them. Adam and Eve understood who they were and embraced their worth and value from within the relationship with God. Now separated from God, Eve would look for her worth and value from her husband. But Adam's heart would no longer be turned toward Eve or God as his relational needs could now be met solely by the work of his hands.

I see this dynamic over and over again in my office, with my friends, in movie themes, etc. A gal sees herself negatively, not able to find qualities and attributes about herself that she likes. She looks for validation and reassurance from her dad, who's often busy with his career and "important" activities. She then turns to romantic relationships to prop up her low self-esteem. Usually the boyfriend initially showers her with affirming words and attentive actions. Soon, however, he sees her emotional neediness exceeds what he's able or wants to contribute. When he walks away, the gal's belief in her lack of value is reaffirmed.

Guys generally like who they are, feel pretty competent about their skills and abilities, and create a life based around their comfort zone. Most guys I talk to cannot understand why gals are so emotionally "needy" and personalize everything. They don't look forward to deep conversations about what they feel and who they are. Guys just wake up and go about their day, living primarily in the present moment. For us gals, that lifestyle causes us to feel a lack of connectedness and we personalize it by feeling neglected, abandoned, and rejected.

Once the connection to God was gone, humankind needed to learn how to love well on our own. Important relational skills needed to be re-learned such as communicating needs, listening to each other without becoming defensive, and moving toward each other when hurt or angry. Without direct access to God's compassion, empathy, grace, and forgiveness, Adam and Eve must have begun to distance from each other. I can draw this conclusion both from personal and general human experience, but also from looking at the account of Cain and Abel. Children learn from the relational model they see at home. It seems pretty clear that Cain did not know how to communicate and process his hurtful feelings towards his brother and God.

I wish I could have heard what Adam and Eve told their boys about God and their actions in the Garden. Did they take responsibility for their decisions or did they continue to blame each other? What we do know is that each son had a different view of God which showed up in their sacrificial presentation. Abel evidenced his reverent heart attitude by bringing the best sacrifice to God. Cain, however, seemed to be resentful from the beginning. Maybe he was angry at missing out on the positive benefits of living in the Garden. Maybe he thought God judged Adam and Eve too harshly and he was bitter, believing the lies the serpent told about God's tainted motives.

Apparently the last straw was God's acceptance of Abel's sacrifice that particular day. Genesis 4:7 says God came to Cain and begged him to see sin crouching at his heart's door. Here we see God's heart of love for humankind despite our rejection of Him. Even though they no longer lived in the Garden, God still pursued the children He loved. Instead of moving toward God and examining his own heart, Cain became violently angry. Since Cain could not take out his rage on God, he took it out on his brother. There's nothing in the text to suggest Cain mourned his murderous actions or repented and honestly admitted his anger was actually at God. Instead, Cain complained that God's punishment was severe and unjustified. Even in the face of such selfishness, God still loved him well by putting a mark on him so Cain would not live his life in fear of being harmed. This action tells me we can trust that by his character, God will always be relational towards us, even when we cannot or chose not to respond relationally to Him.

When Adam and Eve were cut off from all the goodness of God, it negatively affected the physical world and our physical bodies as well. To me, the account of Cain is the first evidence of a person being fundamentally broken. In my definition, broken people have either lost or were born with (and never developed) the capacity to form a relational connection. They do not value the feelings of anyone other than themselves; therefore, they can treat others cruelly without feelings of remorse.

Genesis fast forwards in time and shows us what happened when this brokenness spread through the land.

The Lord saw how great man's wickedness on the earth had become, and that every inclination of the thoughts of his heart was only evil all the time. (Genesis 6:5 NIV)

In a comparably short amount of time, humankind become so broken that the Lord was grieved and filled with pain that he had even created life (Genesis 6:6). How heartbreaking for God, whose sole purpose in creating us was to teach us to love. God decided to give humankind one more chance to choose a lifestyle of love, and he sent the flood to cleanse the earth of its brokenness.

Once the ark came to rest, God lovingly began protecting humankind from themselves by giving Noah, Moses, and Abraham guidelines and commandments designed to show us our need for God. Kind of a reverse psychology approach. By trying to live up to a set of behavioral standards we could never meet, we would hopefully recognize the futility of figuring it out on our own.

For I have the desire to do what is good, but I cannot carry it out. For what I do is not the good I want to do; no, the evil I do not want to do -- this I keep on doing." Romans 7:18-19 NIV.

We hear Paul's frustration and confession that in and of himself, he cannot live life well. Such an admission leads him to the truth that Jesus Christ came to free us from striving to follow the law so we can live according to the Relational model. This model is based on continuously communicating with God about our self-protective barriers. It's humbling and embarrassing when I get those light bulb moments and a blind spot is brought to my attention. My first reaction is to defend and cover up -- exactly what Adam and Eve did in the Garden of Eden. But these days I want to receive healing more than I need to hide so I've learned how to endure the initial anxiety and welcome the revelation.

Unfortunately, not everyone wants God to be Lord over all. Those who prize power quickly learned how to distort God's guidelines and commandments in a manipulative way to gain authority and control for themselves. God institutes leaders to safeguard and guide us in our understanding of loving each other. But many human leaders have used their positions and power to oppress those around them. Sometimes it was accomplished through force in the form of dictatorships and kingdoms. Other times it's been more subtle, accomplished by controlling who was allowed to read and insisting that only religious intermediaries could speak to God. Such rules gave room for the possibility that the religious interpretation given aligned with the leader's own personal or political goals. We still see signs of such manipulation in both direct and indirect ways today.

Outcome-Based Model

One of the most detrimental counterfeits to the Relational system is the Outcome-based model. It promises a direct correlation between working hard and reaching goals. If I work 18 hours a day, 7 days a week, the Outcome-based formula tells me I will receive all the benefits of the "American Dream." On its surface, striving to reach goals and benchmarks appears to be helpful and motivating. That's why this model is enticing. It's much more convenient to independently meet our own needs without relying on God! The "health and wealth" theology uses this same formulaic approach. If I pray and believe hard enough that God wants me to be blessed in specific ways, then God has no choice but to make it happen.

In the Relational model, each person invests in helping one another grow and prosper in loving God, themselves, and others. The Outcome-based model preys on the fear that our legitimate needs will not be met and offers a counterfeit solution to a manufactured problem. Just look at how products are marketed. Instead of focusing on the qualities of a product and letting the consumer decide what they need, commercials appeal to our emotional vulnerabilities. We're told there's a direct correlation between wanting to be loved, accepted, admired, etc. and a particular product. As I looked closer at this model, I began asking probing questions.

> Where did these formulaic equations come from? Who's actually benefiting from me agreeing with them? Do they lead me closer to God or farther away?

What I uncovered was how humankind distorted the godly principle of relational leadership. We replaced it with a system that could be used to manipulate and control for selfish gain.

God's leadership style is repeated throughout the Davidic Psalms: *"His love endures forever."* Leadership without sacrificial love eventually becomes self-centered and punitive. The Bible shows how exasperating and difficult it was for God to lead households and nations of stiff-necked, stubborn, immature people. Trying to lead when you're immature in loving relationally is exhausting and potentially tempting.

Humankind decided to create a shortcut and instituted their own leadership model. Most Outcome-based leaders tell us what goals are godly and institute a set of rules and standards designed to reach those self-determined one-size-fits-all goals. In this model, there's always a set of negative consequences for broken rules or unmet goals.

God gave us the Ten Commandments to show humankind the futility of using rules to replace relationship. What God wants most is for us to draw near to Him so He can draw near to us. Jesus cried over Jerusalem like a mother hen cries over her missing baby chicks. Our worth and value can only be understood through our soul connecting with our creator. When human leadership creates a general set of standards, it leads us away from God's heart and we lose our personhood.

Outcome-based systems connect value and worth directly to achievements. In many homes, schools, churches, small groups, etc., you must follow the rules or meet specified goals in order to receive approval and be recognized as valuable, competent, or good. Not living up to those expectations means letting people down, an unthinkable sin.

You can see this system play out from the first day a child attends school and is asked to measure up on a standardized test. Who decides what facts and theorems are necessary for a student to be "successful" in life? In church and family households, often there are rigid rules to follow and mandated behavior and belief expectations that must be followed. Oftentimes when the system is questioned, the answer given is "because I said so" or the questioner is scolded because their actions reflect badly on the institution or family name. At work, there are sales goals, productivity expectations, time limits, etc., all of which dictate the employee's worth to the company.

I'm not taking issue with setting up systems to encourage people to grow individually and contribute to the community. The Bible talks a lot about having a vision and pressing onward to run the race well. But when humankind use their own standards to judge worth and value, we are putting ourselves in the place of God.

There can be an internal and external tug-of-war when we're conditioned from childhood to connect our character, worth, and value to pleasing someone or meeting goals set by someone else. If an authority figure we respect uses guilt and shame to ensure compliance, we get a warped view of what God expects from us. When Adam and Eve chose independence over relationship with God, humankind learned how to deeply hurt each other. Rather than focusing on ways to support, encourage, and care, people became objects to use and manipulate for personal gain.

God's leadership centers on modeling servant leadership, sacrifice, and unconditional love. The God of the Old Testament was angered, disappointed, and saddened by each human generation who didn't respond to this type of leadership. God wanted them to see how he personally cared for them and understood their needs.

The Israelites looked around, saw every other nation had a human king, and asked God to appoint a king over them. In 1 Samuel 8, God warns Israel through Samuel that a king would draft sons into the military and use their land and energy to supply the military with food and weapons. Their daughters would be expected to take care of the military, people would become slaves, and everyone would be required to give a tenth of their crops and animals to the king. Samuel begged them to consider the cost of Outcome-based leadership, but the Israelites were adamant.

> But the people refused to listen to Samuel. 'No!' they said. 'We want a king over us. Then we will be like all the other nations with a king to lead us and to go out before us and fight our battles.' (1 Samuel 8:19-20 NIV)

All of history shows God's words to be true. Humans have created hierarchical systems based on power, control, and authority which have generally been used to provide a framework for the strong to make others conform to their wishes. It also provides a rationalization to weigh the value of an individual against survival of the system, usually languaged in some magnanimous way. We've all heard mottos like, "The needs of the many outweigh the needs of a few." In the world's system, there must always be a choice. The saddest thing of all is that most of us believe there's no other way to live. But when we view life within a relational context, God gives both sides an opportunity to learn, grow, and mature. No one ends up on the losing end unless they choose, like the Israelites, to tell God no. Even in that instance, God had a plan to bring them to repentance.

Cost of Living in an Outcome-Based System

Another one of my favorite movies is *The Matrix* because it beautifully portrays this tug-of-war. Its basic premise is that the world known by most humans is actually a simulation created by living machines to manipulate and control humanity for their own benefit. Computer hacker Neo begins to find and question computer anomalies and he's recruited by a band of truth-seekers. The most important scene in the movie is when Morpheus tells Neo he has the choice to open his eyes to the simulation. Morpheus warns Neo if he chooses to see the truth, he cannot go back to ignorance. Such an immense decision reveals Neo's character. Does he want to shut his eyes to seeing the world in bondage and continue to do what is best for him or is he motivated by truth, even if it means personal hardship and fighting against oppression?

Neo chooses to take the truthful red pill and when he wakes up, he finds himself attached to an electrical machine by an elaborate cable system. This is what reality looked like for those humans who were enslaved in the dream simulation. Reality was not as pretty as the dream world, but embracing it showed strength and integrity. Neo makes it his life's work to help the Zion brotherhood bring truth to the world. The movie shows another man named Cyber who decides he's tired of living in reality and schemes to return to the matrix so he can live a comfortable, pretend lifestyle. Like Judas, Cyber betrays the Zion brotherhood to the enemy machines for his own benefit.

The price for embracing the Outcome-based system is a life of fear and despair. Life is a never-ending worry cycle that you won't measure up. Every day you work feverishly to reach a goal set by someone else and when you do, you work even harder to stay ahead of the curve. This cycle eventually ends with you crashing in despair, wondering what makes life worthwhile.

We keep insanely believing that doing the same things will bring about a different result. Instead, we need to question the beliefs on which we base our life efforts. In his book *Happier*, Tal Ben-Shahar, Ph.D. talks about training with the Israeli national squash team when he was 16 years old. At that time, he believed winning the championship was necessary for him to feel fulfilled and fulfillment was essential for happiness. He did win and as he savored the mountain-top happy feeling, the everyday emptiness came flooding back.

> *I was befuddled and afraid. The tears of joy shed only hours earlier turned to tears of pain and helplessness. For if I was not happy now, when everything seemed to have worked out perfectly, what prospects did I have of attaining lasting happiness?...But as the days and months unfolded, I did not feel happier; in fact, I was growing even more desolate as I began to see that simply substituting a new goal -- winning the world championship, say --- would not in itself lead me to happiness. Ben-Shahar, Happier, p. 4.*

At some point, every person asks the question, *"Is this all there is to life?"* We may ask it when we're at the top of the mountain or in a deep pit from which we never seem to climb out of -- but we all ask it. The Outcome-based, logical strategy dangles the carrot, telling us to pull up our boots and to put in extra effort and time. It promises if we work hard, we can achieve all our dreams. Has that been true in your life? For me, all that hard work left me burned out and exhausted.

For Christians, this strategy usually means we throw ourselves into church and ministry. We desperately seek emotional highs during worship and obsessively spend our time giving to others. But even these "good" things leave us feeling exhausted, empty, incompetent, worthless, and desperate for happiness and joy. In such a place, we are vulnerable to manipulation and self-destruction. Rather than continuing to do more, why not re-evaluate your life strategy?

My clients laugh at how I talk about loving my bed the way most women love chocolate. Waking up in the morning, I relish the firmness of the mattress and how my body feels rested and refreshed. I stretch like a contented kitty and laughingly make invisible "snow angels" under the sheets. It's such a little, inconsequential thing in the big picture of life. But such contentedness spurs me to prayers of thankfulness for how my life has been transformed in only a few short years. Living an Outcome-based lifestyle meant enduring never-ending fear, self-protection, bitterness, and resentment.

How do you know which system you are living in? Pray Psalm 51 and ask God to show you if any of these Outcome-based themes are present in your heart and mind on a regular basis:

- ○ *Blaming others*
- ○ *Refusing to take responsibility for one's own issues*
- ○ *Living in learned helplessness*
- ○ *Taking on the identity of a martyr*
- ○ *Giving up on life, living in despair and hopelessness*
- ○ *Attempting to fix others through manipulative techniques*
- ○ *Demanding obedience while denying personhood*
- ○ *Denying the role of emotions*

- ○ *Striving to be independent rather than interdependent*
- ○ *Living life as Martha instead of Mary*
- ○ *Choosing to prioritize ministry at the expense of relationships*
- ○ *Denying immaturities and defending them to others*
- ○ *Refusing to allow others to know you for fear of being hurt*
- ○ *Creating rules legislating worth, value and acceptance*

I embrace being filled with the fullness of God and having the opportunity to pour that out on my clients daily in my office. Where I once hated to wake up in the morning because it would be another heavy, busy, demanding day full of disappointment and despair, I now absolutely love my life. Yes, I have hard days with frustrations and difficulties. However, I am committed to knowing in my soul the truth of God's heart. It's a gut knowing that surpasses head knowledge, giving me a godly viewpoint of life where I'm able to see truth and move toward it in every area of my life. This Relational lifestyle brings the happiness and joy every human being was created to desire.

REFLECTION QUESTIONS

1. What do you think God created humankind?
2. How does that belief shape your view of who God is and how he feels about you?
3. Do you love yourself as well as you love others?
4. How do you process feeling like God is disappointed or upset with you?
5. What is your heart motivation when you ask God hard questions?
6. In what ways do you equate value and worth with following rules and standards?

7. Which model do you primarily live out, Relational or Outcome-based?
8. How do you pursue happiness?
9. What Outcome-based themes are present in your life?
10. How does fear keep you from living a Relational life?

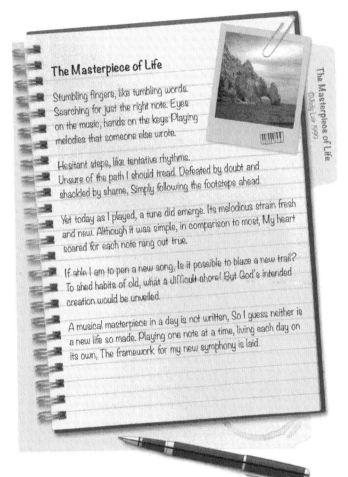

The Masterpiece of Life

Stumbling fingers, like tumbling words.
Searching for just the right note. Eyes
on the music, hands on the keys. Playing
melodies that someone else wrote.

Hesitant steps, like tentative rhythms.
Unsure of the path I should tread. Defeated by doubt and
shackled by shame, Simply following the footsteps ahead.

Yet today as I played, a tune did emerge. Its melodious strain fresh
and new. Although it was simple, in comparison to most, My heart
soared for each note rang out true.

If able I am to pen a new song, Is it possible to blaze a new trail?
To shed habits of old, what a difficult chore! But God's intended
creation would be unveiled.

A musical masterpiece in a day is not written, So I guess neither is
a new life so made. Playing one note at a time, living each day on
its own, The framework for my new symphony is laid.

CHAPTER 4

The Transformation Process

I've always loved C.S. Lewis' *Chronicles of Narnia* books. On the surface, they're exciting adventure stories. But the storylines and characters are also metaphors for deep transformative themes. In *Voyage of the Dawn Treader*, Lewis allows us to identify with our immature human nature through a boy named Eustace. Dragged to Narnia against his will, Eustace wanders off from his cousins on an island, coming across a dead dragon's treasure. Rather than being excited to share the discovery with everyone, Eustace rationalizes how the others have treated him badly and decides to keeps the treasure all for himself. He slips on a golden bracelet and takes a nap on top of the treasure. When he wakes up, Eustace finds he has transformed into a dragon. At first he revels in his size and strength, enjoying frightening the group with his flames and talons. But after a while, Eustace begins feeling isolated and lonely.

Sitting on a heap of gold blaming others for his circumstances doesn't bring Eustace any comfort. Eustace decides to magnanimously overlook everyone's faults because he hates feeling lonely. He searches for a way to peel the dragon skin off so he can return to being a boy. But all his self-serving, frantic actions only cause him more physical pain. His anger compounds the resentment towards those who, in his opinion, did this to him. Eventually Eustace chooses to look at his own actions and heart attitude, seeing clearly how he failed to love anyone other than himself.

It wasn't until Eustace reaches this point of humility that Aslan comes to him. Like King David, Eustace confesses to Aslan how his self-protective, immature, selfishness got him into this mess and how his attempts to cover it up made things worse. Aslan asks if Eustace truly wants to gain a new life as a boy, letting him know the cost he would pay. Eustace steels himself for the painful process of Aslan ripping away all the relational barriers his selfish immaturity has created. The initial pain gives way to a strength and trust in Aslan that makes enduring the difficult process possible. Once he has returned to his human form, Eustace tentatively asks his cousins to forgive him, unsure of their reaction. His repentance quickly ushers in a time of celebration as Eustace is happily incorporated into the family fold.

Barriers to Transformation

The transformation process begins with asking God to reveal all the self-protective hurdles that prevent you from living out a mature life strategy. This can be a slow, painful process. Our template for the transformative process begins in Psalm 51. David's purpose in writing these words was not to make promises about changing his ways, to put the blame on Bathsheba, to beat himself up for being a terrible man, or to justify his actions. It wasn't even about his sorrow in lusting after Bathsheba and killing her husband. Instead, David asks God to show him all the sinful barriers that separate him from God. He's heartbroken to see his failure to love well and earnestly prays for God to create in him a pure heart. David knew his hurtful actions stemmed from a selfish, immature heart that needed healing.

The sacrifices of God are a broken spirit; a broken and contrite heart, O God you will not despise. (Psalm 51:17 NIV)

Most human beings do not willingly pray Psalm 51 every day and ask God to show them the brokenness in their heart. To do so, we must be willing to look at hard, scary, painful feelings, decisions, and actions. Oftentimes, it's only when we're in dire, difficult, gut-wrenching pain and catastrophic circumstances that we find strength and courage to pray such a Psalm. That's why clients keep coming to my office every week for months, sometimes even for years. It's so difficult to keep our own heart open in this process, even when we know it's necessary. Throughout the counseling session, I'm redirecting clients back to painful wounds and feelings of shame, embarrassment, anger, and sadness. God designed healing to take place when we choose to become vulnerable in the presence of a caring, accepting, safe person. I see this principle illustrated in the account of the prodigal son.

Jesus used parables as a way to illustrate the differences between godly principles and immature human behaviors. The prodigal son, like Adam and Eve, decided he wanted to make his own choices about his life and have control over his own destiny. He brazenly asked his father for the inheritance he would receive when his father died. I wonder what the prodigal son missed in the relationships at home that he needed to go out into the world looking for something else. Did he feel put down by his older brother or ignored by his father? Most likely he had unprocessed disappointments that kept him from receiving all that his father provided for him. Otherwise, he never would have needed to try and fill such an emotional void with unhealthy people and activities.

The prodigal son focused solely on what he was missing, causing him to leave the people who loved him dearly. He gravitated towards those who only cared about using him for his money. When we're unable to move towards people because of deep hurt, it leaves us vulnerable to those who prey on lost souls.

When the son had spent all he had, a famine came, putting him in a horrible situation. The "friends" he had surrounded himself with were gone. Selfishness shows its true colors when we no longer have anything of value to offer. These users either punish us for what we no longer bring to them or disappear, leaving us alone to our fate.

The prodigal son was now in desperate need and anxiously realized he had messed up big time. When we get that "oh no" feeling, most of us jump from the frying pan into the fire -- and the prodigal son did just that. He found a job feeding pigs, but his employer was as much a user as his friends. Hard hearted and unsympathetic, the employer would not even allow the prodigal son to eat the same pods he fed the pigs.

Luke 15:17 NIV says, *"When he came to his senses...."* How many of us have been in that same place! Sometimes it takes a long period of time under significant duress before we reach out. When we take our focus off ourselves and put it onto God, we can be overwhelmed by the huge hole we've dug for ourselves. It's human nature to panic and want to be rescued. That's why it's so difficult to choose long term transformation over immediate relief. I often tell my clients my prayer is they choose to BE better rather than FEEL better. Had the prodigal son been rescued at that moment, he probably would've landed right back in similar circumstances a short time later. Transformation requires insight, confession, grieving, and vision -- all of which take time and work.

I see the same cycle with abused women after bad fights or addicts who swear they won't use again after a close call. It takes more than just wanting to be out of a bad situation for healing and change to occur. That's why most of the time being rescued by friends/family is not the answer. Instead, God leads us through three important stages of transformation.

Stages of Transformation

Heart & Character Examination

God asks us to fearfully, but determinedly, examine our heart and our character. Once God pulls back the curtain of denial and exposes our brokenness, most people immediately go into fix-it mode. Every one of us hopes we can get that valuable piece of missing information which allows us to solve our problems quickly so we can live happily-ever-after. Problem solving's an important skill, but when we use it to avoid sitting with God, it's just another unhealthy self-protective strategy.

When the prodigal son finally pulled his head out of the sand and looked at his perilous situation, he jumped right into problem solving mode. Remembering how his father treated his servants well, the son decided he would ask his father for a job. The account doesn't ever say the prodigal son had a change of heart at this point. Instead of searching his heart and character to see what he was lacking, the son focused on coming up with a good enough sounding speech that would convince his father to give him a job. It doesn't record any soul searching by the son about how much his father showed love to him by giving him his inheritance early. There's no account of this son grieving the sorrow he caused his father by his words and actions. It appears the prodigal son only focused on getting his own needs met. And that's the problem with a non-relational approach to life, it's selfish, unloving, and unfulfilling.

It's been said the definition of insanity is doing the same thing over and over expecting a different result. The greatest enemy to transformation is the belief that we can achieve the abundant life if we just work harder, understand more, communicate better, or come up with a more effective plan. That belief is a lie. Paul's writings in Romans and Galatians talk about putting such a belief to death and embracing a relational life strategy. Choosing to examine our heart and character is essential to transformation.

Responding to Truth

When we allow God to change our paradigm, it causes us to look at ourselves and our life in a completely different light. Most folks are overwhelmed with feelings of failure for not having seen the truth earlier. Our learned response to failure is self-condemnation. Feeling stupid, embarrassed, and disappointed causes us to push away from God and others. That's because we've adopted the human Outcome-based view of learning rather than God's Relational approach. When we view life as a process, we have an expectation that God will continually reveal things to us over time. God works with each one of us in our own individual timeframe. He doesn't set one-size-fits-all standards.

I see some of this language in the prodigal son's speech when he tells his father he's no longer worthy to be his son.

> **That statement is all about how the son negatively sees himself and has nothing to do with the son seeing what is true about the father.**

In a relational exchange, the son would share how his own issues blind him from seeing his father clearly and how grieved he is to now see the truth. King David shows us the healthy response to conviction is to take our feelings to God and ask him to change our heart. David's approach to God is not one of martyrdom or abasing himself, but just agreeing with God about his immaturities.

Other unhealthy responses include negative comparisons, rationalizations, minimizing, and blame shifting. In an outcome-based society, showing weakness brings ridicule and hurt. Mankind has learned how to employ self-protective responses to shield themselves from non-relational consequences. A significant hurdle in the transformation process is our fear that God will reject us when we show immaturities. I continually pray for courage and strength for myself and my clients to seek God when we see our weaknesses. Choosing faith in God's heart for us over and over empowers us to hurdle these barriers.

Living in Hope

Transformation allows us to build a solid, godly foundation on which we live our daily life. Jesus told a parable about a man who built his house upon the sand and when a storm came, it was washed away. When we build our life on self-protective strategies and employ punitive, self-condemning responses, we're building a house on a shaky foundation. Freedom comes from knowing God is excited to show us how to build strategies that can withstand difficult life circumstances and emotional roller coasters.

Living out of truth means cultivating an excitement and passion to see and connect with God in our everyday life. It's impossible to be passionate without hope. Unfortunately, mankind has learned how to beat hope down to a manageable size. We're allowed to dream about things that are "reasonable" or "practical," but to hope for the stars is considered unrealistic and crazy. Such a life strategy is based on managing fear. In 2 Timothy 1:7 we're told not to live a life out of timidity and fear.

Just as darkness must give way to light, fear must give way when we choose to allow hope into our heart.

Hope that God does really love us. Hope that our life can be different. Hope that we can trust in God and others. Hope that God wants us to live life as an adventure.

Fear of disappointment is the enemy of hope. How many times have you wanted to be excited about a potential new job or the outcome of a relationship, but didn't want to set yourself up for disappointment? One way we put a lid on hope is believing we shouldn't burden others. Mistakenly, we believe keeping our needs to a minimum and not imposing too much on others will keep us from being disappointed. We see an example of this belief when the prodigal son chose to only ask his father to become a servant rather than returning to sonship. He had a completely mistaken view of himself and his father.

His father had been waiting and watching for his son to come home. Rather than being angry and holding a grudge, the father felt loving compassion and ran to his son, kissing and hugging him. Yes, there were barriers they needed to address, but the father wanted his son to hope into a full restoration of the relationship rather than settling for something less.

I believe it was at that moment that the son was able to clearly see the truth about his father's heart. David often speaks in the Psalms about how loving kindness brings us to repentance. True repentance only happens when our heart connects with the heart of God. As the son begins to recite his prepared speech, I believe he now speaks from a different place. Opening up to receive his father's genuine loving welcome changed the son's heart. It gave him the courage to see and confess his own brokenness, but also hope into change.

I can't give you a list of "5 Easy Steps to Transformation" nor can I tell you exactly what it looks like when transformation takes place. What I can say is there's a shift in your soul when you move from a place of needing self-protective, condemning life strategies that lock you into fear. You will feel the difference in living a life strategy that embraces the freedom to be vulnerable and passionate.

> Transformation is not a one-time event, but a progressive revelation that will continue to unfold throughout our lifetime.

Transformation in Narnia

I love watching the process of transformation in the lives of my clients. Helping them seek God's path for them is an honor. Clients find it helpful to have a variety of examples illustrating how the process unfolds. I've been inspired by the transformative process found in C.S. Lewis' story *The Lion, Witch and the Wardrobe.*

We initially get to know the Pevensie siblings during World War II when they're shipped off by train out of London to an estate in the countryside. Watching the children interact, we get an understanding of their personalities and relational conflicts. The oldest girl, Susan, is the mother figure, admonishing them all to be proper and follow the rules. Edmund is sullen and angry. He defies Susan's dictates and is hostile to older brother Peter's authority. Lucy loves all her older siblings unconditionally and has a sensitive, caring heart and manner.

Whether by happenstance or providence, the children find themselves in the land of Narnia when they hide out in a large closet. Expecting to be crammed into a small, tight space, they find themselves in a strange land where it's always winter. Thus begins their transformative journey from immature children to empowered, confident rulers of Narnia.

Lucy visits Narnia prior to the other siblings and makes a friend named Mr. Tumnus. Mr. Tumnus connects with Lucy's genuine caring heart over a cup of tea. He sacrificially makes the choice to disobey the White Queen's order to turn in any humans found in the land. When all the children arrive in Narnia, they're told Mr. Tumnus has been arrested by the White Queen for his disobedience. Lucy's selflessness, loyalty, and compassion are evident as she insists they must find a way to rescue him.

Edmund previously followed Lucy into Narnia, but lied about it to Peter and Susan. The White Queen promised Edmund if he brought all his siblings to her castle, she'd make him a king to rule over them. For the price of his favorite candy and the dream of revenge, Edmund agrees to do so. We can see the difference in heart attitude between Mr. Tumnus and Edmund. Both are offered the same choice, but they respond in very different ways. Their outward decisions reflect the internal struggle between self-protection and sacrificial love.

Many times we, like Edmund, harbor resentment and bitterness toward someone who has hurt us. Rather than learning to sit in the hurt and receive comfort, we allow it to impact our ability to see clearly. The White Queen made the offer to Edmund not for his benefit, but for hers. Blinded by his immaturity, Edmund was vulnerable to the predatory schemes of the evil Queen.

The other three children are approached by a talking beaver who tells them of a prophecy that states four humans will be used by Aslan to defeat the White Queen's hold on Narnia. I find Peter's response very telling. He replies that the prophecy could not possibly relate to him because he's just a boy from Finchley. This statement reveals Peter has no understanding of his capabilities, his heart, and his strength of character. Peter sees himself through the lens of his human frailties and weaknesses rather than who God created him to be.

I, too, used to look at myself as "just Judy," another overweight, middle-aged mom from Columbus, Ohio. Most of my life I couldn't imagine what God found special about me. I certainly didn't see anything good when I looked in the mirror. "God don't make no junk" was a common saying in the 1970s. Intellectually I knew I was supposedly valuable because God created me. But that knowledge made me feel even worse because I couldn't emotionally believe that message. My self-protective strategies kept me from being able to confess the ways I kept myself weak rather than hope for change.

Thankfully God loved me too much to let me sit in despair. The Holy Spirit whispered to my heart, stirring up longing. I kept looking in the mirror, journaling, and talking to safe people. Head knowledge is not enough; truth needs to be fueled by the heart and soul.

The Song of Songs illustrates how God woos our heart. The Beloved's heart begins to receive what her Bridegroom says is true about her. She uses that knowledge to passionately pursue him, pushing past all obstacles to reach his side. At the beginning of the book, she worries about how she looks and what the bridegroom thinks of her. By the end, the bride talks joyously about her worth and boldly offers all she has become to her Bridegroom. The bride went through a roller coaster of thoughts and emotions in this maturing process. The bridegroom used each step to purge her of fear so she could embrace his love.

When offered the opportunity for growth, Susan responds out of fear. She blames Peter for bringing them to such a dangerous place and berates herself for not controlling the situation. Again, at times I see this attitude in myself. Like Susan, I feel safer with structure and predictability. This is one of those personality hardwiring traits God instilled in me. I like to be creatively free within very clear parameters. When circumstances would change or I couldn't predict outcomes, I used to become overwhelmed with anxiety. I'd keep running "what if" scenarios through my head before and after events and conversations, beating myself up for not handling things better.

God prompted important people in my life to confront me in love about the cost of living in fear. I believed the lie that if I worked hard enough, planned efficiently, and trusted only in myself I'd feel safe and secure. God gently, yet firmly, helped me admit how I had chosen to trust in fear instead of hoping into God's heart for me. Since that revelation, I have had many, many chances to choose faith rather than fear. I've learned to withstand the initial anxiety, anchoring to the solid foundation of knowing God intimately rather than grasping at empty theological concepts.

Pivotal Moments of Growth

The Narnia story continues when it's discovered that Edmund is headed for the White Queen's castle. Peter and Susan are angry at being forced to take on the responsibility of rescuing Edmund. As they resentfully chase after Edmund, we watch them begin to take the focus off blaming their brother and turn to examining their own hearts and motives.

There's a captivating, pivotal scene in the movie illustrating Peter's growth in maturity and character. Peter, Susan, and Lucy are walking across a frozen river that's beginning to thaw. They're surrounded by the White Queen's agents, one of whom echoes Peter's prior words by telling him this is not his fight and suggesting he just return to Finchley and resume his old life.

All that had happened in Narnia went through Peter's mind in a split second. He was free to go back to the security of his old life. Or, he could take a risk and press forward toward the hope he would actually be transformed into a King of Narnia. My heart soars and I get goose bumps every time I watch Peter plunge his sword into the ice, causing the siblings to be on an iceberg that carries them forward toward Aslan.

At that point they didn't know much about Aslan or how to stand and fight against the White Queen. Peter grabs the opportunity to become the man he envisions, even though it involves hardship and suffering. That's the choice God puts before each one of us throughout our transformation process. Do we choose to defend, rationalize, minimize, and live in a spirit of timidity or do we hang onto our mustard seed of faith and leap into hope?

There was a time in my life when I experienced a significant depression. I found it hard to get out of bed, function at work, maintain my household, and care for my family. I kept playing a song by Ray Boltz that talked about how God gives us back our tomorrows even after we've thrown them away. I'd sob while listening to the words. Not only had God given me much and I'd messed it up, but for a long time I didn't know if I even wanted to put in the work it would take to heal and change. God reminded me the Apostle Paul was a man who also experienced a tug-of-war about his spiritual walk. He led me to Romans 5:4-5 NIV, which gave me the courage to press into the hard emotional work.

> But we also rejoice in our sufferings, because we know that suffering produces perseverance; perseverance, character; and character, hope. And hope does not disappoint us, because God has poured out his love into our hearts by the Holy Spirit, whom he has given us.

God promised if I allowed him to open up the place in my heart where I'd stored all my suffering, He would strengthen me, transform my character, and give me hope. And that's exactly what God did. He brought people alongside who saw me clearly through God's eyes when I couldn't see myself. They encouraged me to keep my head down and persevere in cleaning out the hurt, pain, lies, and self-protective strategies while they kept sharing the vision of where God was leading me.

It was actually really helpful not to feel guilty about my lack of hope while I was struggling to walk through the painful valley. I disagree with sermons that make folks feel guilty about not having hope in the midst of difficult circumstances. Being able to release to others the big picture allowed me to work hard.

After some months of letting painful memories flow out in word and pen, God nudged me to look up and see my growth. With the help of others who knew me well, I saw a new emotional openness with myself and others. I was more genuine in my relationships with less anxiety. Celebrating the internal and external growth brought an overwhelming feeling of gratitude to God. Looking up in thanksgiving allowed a stirring of hope in my heart, spurring me to keep walking out the plan.

Returning to Narnia, the story shows Edmund foolishly entering the White Queen's castle and arrogantly sitting on her throne. When he tells the White Queen his siblings are heading to see Aslan, she reveals her true agenda – the desire to destroy them all. Edmund is thrown into the dungeon where he meets Mr. Tumnus. The White Queen takes great delight in telling Mr. Tumnus that Edmund is the one who betrayed him and his own siblings.

While in prison, Edmund's eyes are opened to the darkness in his own heart. If he continued to live out of selfishness, he'd become just as cruel as the White Queen. At that point in the story, when Edmund is at rock bottom, C.S. Lewis introduces us to hope in Christ through the character of Aslan.

Aslan is portrayed as a great lion. He walks and talks with Peter, Susan, and Lucy, introducing himself and sharing his vision of who they each could become in life. They find him to be wise, loving, and patient; someone to be respected and feared.

The White Queen arrives at Aslan's camp with Edmund as her prisoner. After a private meeting with Aslan, the White Queen states they've come to an agreement and she frees Edmund. Lucy and Susan rush to greet him with welcoming hugs. Shame and embarrassment keep him from looking at Peter. During this journey, however, Peter has grown greatly in loving well. He goes to Edmund and embraces him joyfully.

The next morning Aslan talks with Edmund about his choices. Edmund's demeanor changes drastically as his shame is lifted. He is in the presence of one who sees not only the outward appearance, but also the repentant heart of a true believer. How sweet it is to allow God to replace shame with mercy and grace.

This part of the story brings tears every time as I join with Edmund in remembering the ways I've hurt others out of my own unresolved pain and immaturity. Years ago I became an integral part of a church. I helped out in the nursery, co-led a Bible study, prayed for people at the end of the service, and sang on the worship team. When I wasn't singing up front, I was in the back putting the words up on the screen during the service. At that time, I was still anxious about being criticized by authority figures. My worth and value were connected to approval and I made sure no one could accuse me of doing anything wrong.

One day I received a call from the Assistant Pastor stating I'd made someone uncomfortable while praying for them on Sunday. The Assistant Pastor wanted to schedule a meeting. Immediately I went into anxiety defense mode. I was angry the complainant didn't come directly to me about the situation and give me an opportunity to explain myself. Feeling judged and condemned, I hated being called into "the principal's office." That horrible "I'm in trouble" feeling makes me crazy because I know it's a trigger button from my childhood. I hate when it invades my present and I can't make it stop.

All these complicated feelings surrounded me. I had no ability or energy to press into them with the Assistant Pastor so I walked out, leaving gaping holes at the church for others to fill. The painful knowledge that I was hurting people pushed me to seek healing for the triggered wounds. Writing these words makes me wince at my immaturity, but I also feel God's loving kindness for the painful place I was in at that time.

What the process looked like for me was a lot of grieving over the gap between who I wanted to be and where I was currently. God opened up memories of past times where I'd been hurt but hadn't grieved the impact of those hurts in my life. I spent several days journaling and venting my anxiety and anger to a close friend. She encouraged me to pour out all my fear and insecurities, then lovingly redirected my focus back to God. He showed me how choosing to protect myself kept me feeling angry and scared. If I wanted the "in trouble" button removed, I needed to learn how to be vulnerable and not shut down or run away.

A couple of years later, a friend invited me back to that same church for a worship service. I immediately felt a jolt of anxiety, wanting to stay away from any potential encounter with the Assistant Pastor. The friend mentioned the Pastor had left the church shortly after I did. God reminded me how I'd worked hard on my character. He acknowledged my anxiety, but promised if I intentionally pressed into the fear, He'd be able to bless me.

I came late to the service and drove around the parking lot a couple of times, asking God for the courage to face my residual feelings of guilt and shame. Getting out of my car, I was stunned to see the former Assistant Pastor walk across the lot and into the church. Lifting my hands up to heaven I said, "I guess you're throwing me in the deep end tonight God!"

This was my first real test of walking with the Shepherd through the valley of the shadow of death. Did I really believe on the other side of the valley was a banqueting table filled with peace, joy, and grace? I'd always found a way to run or to rationalize, but this time I was determined to walk in and allow myself to feel everything.

Sitting in the back of the room, I concentrated on being emotionally open and vulnerable. At the end of the service, many folks recognized me, giving me warm hugs and saying they'd missed me. Then I saw the Assistant Pastor deliberately head for me and I held my breath. Our relationship had been difficult throughout my time at the church, so I didn't know what to expect.

The first words out of her mouth were, "I'm so sorry about everything." The part of my heart that had been in bondage since that event suddenly broke free, praising God for His goodness to me. I was able to explain my immaturity and ask for her forgiveness, which she received. She shared this was the first time she'd been to the church in a year!

What an amazing blessing God gave me as I chose to walk in faith and trust in His heart. Since that day, there've been many other times when I didn't want to press into emotionally difficult situations, but the blessing I received that day pushes me forward. I know I'll find the strength to grow because experience has shown I always receive more than I sacrifice.

Seeing Growth

One evening shortly after Edmund's return, Lucy and Susan follow Aslan away from the camp and watch, horrified, as Aslan willingly gives himself as a sacrifice to the White Queen on Edmund's behalf. They see him ridiculed and humiliated, then eventually killed. After the enemy leaves, the girls rush down and sit with Aslan's body, weeping and telling him how they love him. A message is sent to Peter and Edmund telling of Aslan's death and the impending assault by the White Queen's army.

Here's another pivotal transformative point in the story. As Peter starts to put on his armor, Edmund tells him the army of Aslan is ready to follow his lead. Peter slumps over, declaring he's incapable of leading an army because he's only a boy from Finchley. Edmund reminds him of all the progress he's made and how he's matured in his understanding of himself.

Once again, Peter has the opportunity to see and acknowledge his growth and move forward into his destined role or to let fear cause him to back down and prioritize his own safety. What causes Peter to pick up his sword is Edmund's heartfelt testimony. Determined to never again bow down to the White Queen, Edmund declares he will sacrifice his life to purchase freedom for the people of Narnia.

We each can live in this world as wounded warriors, sharing our own testimonies of how God has rescued us from our enemies. The Bible talks about the role of encouragement. Inspiring each other with stories of transformation empowers us to run the race and persevere to the end. I always find it exhilarating to hear how God has worked in the lives of others because it reminds me of the vision God has put in my own heart.

As the morning of the epic battle dawns, Susan and Lucy kiss Aslan's dead body one last time and begin to head back to camp. They hear a loud noise and turn around to see the body has disappeared. Bewildered, they run to the stone table calling for Aslan. As in a glorious vision, they see a resurrected Aslan walking towards them. The girls run and joyfully embrace him. Aslan tells them the White Queen doesn't know that sacrificial love is more powerful than death. The girls ride on Aslan's back to the Queen's castle where he sets the captives, including Mr. Tumnus, free and they all head to the battlefield.

I generally skip over fighting scenes in books and movies, however, I find the Narnia battle intensely compelling. Peter, Edmund, and all the Narnian warriors choose to be part of that war out of principle. They know they have no chance of defeating the White Queen with their small band, but they don't back down from doing the right thing.

I love that honorable, noble sentiment and am fiercely adamant about wanting to live my life in that same passionate way. My heart aches at the cruelty and pain the warriors suffer in battle before Aslan arrives. I flinch each time I watch the brave Narnian warriors die and see Edmund mortally wounded. It reminds me of the persecution going on every day in much of the world.

Jesus chose to willingly die on the cross as the ultimate model of loving well. Looking around this broken world with people who hurt others, sometimes intentionally, it can feel like a hopeless battle that cannot be won. I don't know why God allows pain, bloodshed, abuse, etc. If Jesus' death ended his story on earth, then we'd have no basis to believe in God's ability to work all things together for our good. But Jesus' resurrection brings hope into dark places. Hope for today and for eternity, even in the midst of a battlefield. The process of transformation leads to a life worth living in this world and the glorious anticipation of eternity with God.

REFLECTION QUESTIONS

1. What are your barriers to transformation?
2. In what ways do you relate to the prodigal son?
3. Which unhealthy self-protective strategies do you utilize?
4. How do you handle disappointment?
5. Do you see yourself as "just me"?
6. Which Pevensie child do you most reflect and in what ways?
7. Do you have an "in trouble" button?
8. In what ways have you seen growth and transformation?
9. How do you live as a "wounded warrior"?
10. Do you need a renewed sense of hope?

ROADMAP TO FREEDOM

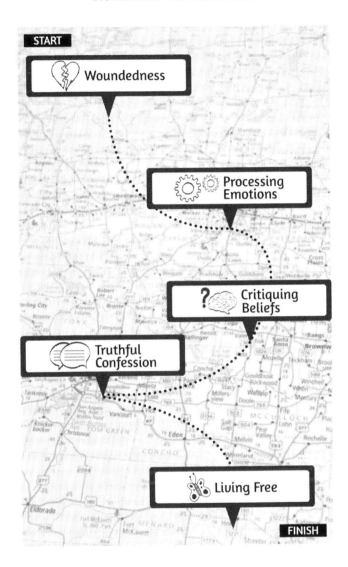

Therapists use outcome-based models to form a diagnosis and apply an applicable treatment plan. The clinical models start with identifying specific symptoms, then show the process of moving from the problem to the solution. The treatment plan lists specific behaviors and suggestions to be given to the client and measurable goals to determine whether treatment is successful. As you well know by now, I do not look at life through that lens. Instead, what I provide my clients is a Roadmap to Freedom.

The remainder of this book is separated into chapters that explain the stages in the transformative journey. Rather than viewing people as problems to be solved, this roadmap guides you through the transformational process. The journey will be unique to each person, but the process is the same.

One of the biggest challenges for my clients is to change how they view success. Traditional treatment plans focus on behavioral milestones to gauge process. Clinicians and clients look at changes in behaviors like highway mile markers telling them how far they need to go to reach their goal. If a client doesn't see progress fast enough, they often blame themselves and either work harder on the same things or give up completely.

Success is measured very differently on the Roadmap to Freedom. Growth in maturity and character comes from experiencing increased freedom and permission to live out personhood. I used to feel I was stuck in a straitjacket with a gag in my mouth around specific people and in certain environments. As I embraced permission to own my feelings and beliefs, I began experiencing less fear and felt more grounded in truth. Those changes came about because God was freeing me from strategies and beliefs that kept my sense of self locked away. The Roadmap to Freedom provides clarity and hope when we feel lost and alone.

CHAPTER 5

Woundedness

I was recently visiting my friend Diane who's expecting her first baby. We looked at the cute baby things she had ready and Diane talked excitedly how she couldn't wait to sing her daughter lullabies as she rocked her to sleep. Then her eyes welled up with tears. "I love this baby so much, but I know I'm going to screw her up and that makes me really sad."

Diane grew up in a verbally abusive household and she dealt with her woundedness by developing an eating disorder. I'm really proud of the progress Diane has made over the last few years. She worked hard to figure out the reason she found it hard to love herself was because she never felt loved by her parents. One of the most important truths Diane came to understand is that everyone is wounded and God does not stop the merry-go-round of life while we heal. Instead, He calls us to focus on our transformation journey, even when that means we continue to negatively impact others. Why?

I don't have an answer for you. What I do know is God promises to be with each of us at all times, whether we're the one doing the wounding or the one being hurt. Looking back over the past 24 years, even the past 24 hours, I can see how my own issues have impacted my ability to love my son as well as I'd like. When I talk to God about my sorrow, He sits in the sadness with me, but then shows me the growth I've made so I have hope for tomorrow. Because I'm able to connect relationally with God's heart for my life, I can entrust to God my son's need for healing.

In Matthew 11:25-30, Jesus says God has revealed himself to little children rather than the wise. I think that's because children have an amazing ability to have faith and trust in adults to care for them without needing to fully understand everything. When Jesus puts out his hand and says he knows I am weary and burdened with sorrow, I do believe He wants to lift the guilt from me and help my son get his own healing. As I shared this truth with Diane, her sorrow and anxiety were replaced with thankfulness and peace.

How We Are Wounded

Sticks and stones can break my bones but words will never hurt me. Unfortunately, that old children's rhyme is completely untrue. Physical abuse, accidents, chronic health issues, etc. leave external evidence of being wounded. Hurtful words are often just as painful and linger in the form of negative beliefs about ourselves. Those wounds are devastating because we can live out the rest of our life believing those lies.

There are fundamental skills, core longings, and needs God places in us from birth. These include being loved, feeling special, being enjoyed, caring for others, wanting to be our own unique person, and living a meaningful life. Research regarding human development has documented fundamental skills and needs necessary for a healthy, happy, and mature life. Erik Erikson, Ph.D. describes it as a series of crises that need to be navigated. If the developmental crisis is not fully resolved, interpersonal and relational wounding occurs. Using *Erikson's Stages of Development*, I created a chart to show the impact of these crises on our woundedness. Look through the Negative Resolution list to see if you can connect your areas of woundedness to different events at different stages of your life.

Impact of Erikson's Psychosocial Stages on Woundedness

Stage	Crisis	Positive Resolution	Negative Resolution
Infancy (0-1 year)	Trust vs. Mistrust	Hope Faith in caregivers Appreciation of interdependence and relatedness Ability to receive love, care & affection	Suspicion Distrust of people Fear of future events Need for predictability Need to protect oneself Unable to attach or bond with others
Early Childhood (1-3 years)	Autonomy vs. Doubt	Embrace personhood Sense of independence Embrace sense of personal control	Shame Self-doubt Indecisive Inability to self-regulate
Play Age (3-6 years)	Initiative vs. Guilt	Self-starter Sense of purpose Humor Empathy Resilience Balance between being a leader and showing cooperation	Guilt Sense of inadequacy Anxiety Easily discouraged Self-protective Needs to be in control to feel safe
School Age (6-12 years)	Industry vs. Inferiority	Competence Problem-solving Humility Secure in oneself Pride in accomplishments	Sense of inferiority Inability to think critically Needs approval and validation Self-hatred

Stage	Crisis	Positive Resolution	Negative Resolution
Teens (12-19 years)	Identity vs. Confusion	Sense of uniqueness and individuality Respect for and tolerance of others	Confusion about self Lack of permission to have own opinions Intimidated by others
Early Adulthood (20-25 years)	Intimacy vs. Isolation	Ability to love sacrificially Ability to make commitments to others	Inability to bond relationally Life characterized by selfish immaturity
Adulthood (26-64 years)	Generativity vs. Stagnation	Focus is on building strong relationships in all areas of life Contributes to the world in personally meaningful ways	Narcissistic approach to life Prioritizes self Unproductive and uninvolved in the world
Aging Years (65-death)	Integrity vs. Despair	Ability to approach life challenges and impending death with integrity Reflects back on life positively	Dissatisfaction with life and relationships Despair over prospect of death Bitterness and regrets

God's plan is for parents to be an integral part of meeting needs, teaching skills, and facilitating their child's journey into their own personhood. This concept is different from the Outcome-based model where parents are judged by others based on whether their child meets certain societal standards. In the Relational Model, the goal of parenting is to help our kids see themselves the way God sees them and to live out of that knowledge. When they do so, they'll learn to make decisions and choices in daily life that lead to a happy, healthy abundant lifestyle. Obviously, parents can only model and give to their family what they have received and/or learned for themselves. When parents fail their child in these ways on a regular basis, wounding occurs and the child employs self-protective coping strategies.

It can be devastating for a child of any age to look back and acknowledge their parents failed them. We're created with the belief our parents will love us unconditionally like our Father in heaven. When we're disappointed, many of us rationalize saying, "They did the best they could." Maybe they did, I'm not here to make a judgment. What I do know, however, is every parent fails their child and every child needs to be able to talk about how they were hurt.

Many times, clients feel like they're betraying a parent if they acknowledge they were failed. But minimizing and covering up the truth eats away at self-esteem and personhood, keeping us broken and helpless. What if you walk across the parking lot after leaving my office and a car comes around the corner and runs you over. It doesn't matter whether the driver did it intentionally or by accident, you need to tell someone you're injured so you can get help. How the driver feels about the incident is between them and God, it's not your responsibility to save or fix the driver's feelings. We don't always need to tell our parents how they hurt us, but we need to be willing to acknowledge it to God.

When 40 year old Sharon recognized God created her to be loved and enjoyed, Sharon was able to acknowledge she didn't receive enough love from her family. That confession allowed her to see how she had mistakenly hoped for those things from each guy who said something nice to her. This process provided Sharon permission to feel compassion for herself instead of guilt. Without that compassion, Sharon was stuck in self-hatred.

Once clients give themselves permission to talk about their injuries, I provide a safe environment to acknowledge their wounds truthfully and learn how to grieve how they were hurt and by whom. That brings context to the pain and permission to ask for and receive care and comfort from God and others. Grace and mercy must be extended to ourselves first before we can release those who have failed us to God through forgiveness. Understanding context validates the emptiness that ends up being played out in self-destructive ways.

Compartmentalization

One of the most helpful models I offer to clients to gain context is the idea of compartmentalization. How many times have you realized you were giving someone attitude like a teenager? Do you have times when you just want to curl up on the couch with your jammies on after a hard day like a little kid? We all find ourselves living out familiar childhood themes. But when those childhood behaviors and self-protective strategies interfere in our adult life, we need to look for the root cause.

I explain compartmentalization as a hallway with different rooms containing different parts of us at different ages. I'm not talking about multiple personality disorder, dissociative identity disorder, or any other specific mental illness. These rooms generally correspond to Erikson's Stages of Development model. If an adult did not experience their parents as attentive to their needs as an infant, they'll have an inner room filled with unmet needs from that time period. When a teenager's not given permission to make mistakes in finding their own identity, they'll have an inner room filled with resentment. If the feelings from this room are not cleaned out, bitterness and rebellion will often be a large part of their adult life. Folks who are unaware of unmet needs and developmental emotional deficits will subconsciously expect others to fill parental roles, putting too much pressure on that relationship.

Jill grew up with a mother suffering from Obsessive Compulsive Disorder. Her father focused most of his time and energy on keeping his wife content, leaving little time for bonding with his daughter. Now in her 30s, Jill shamefully confessed she wants her husband to tell her she looks pretty and to do things like take care of her when she's sick. Jill reported intentionally manipulating him to say and do things that make her feel special.

As we talked about the legitimate core longings God instilled and how those needs went unmet in the early years of her life, it made sense to Jill that her inner little girl still wanted a daddy. Once she understood where the needs were coming from, Jill was able to grieve how her father had failed her. She's now able to recognize when she puts those expectations on her husband and has learned to directly tell him what she needs.

I know when I talk with clients about their inner child, teenager or 20-something parts it's odd languaging, but it gives perspective and context to otherwise confusing feelings, thoughts, and behaviors. When my son Ben was playing high school baseball, I'd sit in the stands near the high school teenagers rather than with the other parents. On those days, I'd spend a lot of time on my appearance, wanting to be seen as "cool." One game I even jumped into a conversation between some teens in front of me. They looked at me like I was a space alien! Add that to my new obsession with pink, sparkly accessories and I thought I was going crazy! My counselor gave me this compartmentalization model. It allowed me to pinpoint where I had inner parts that needed God's healing.

Self-protective survival strategies are essential for children to make sure their core personhood is not crushed when they have no ability to take themselves out of a harmful environment. God protects us when we're emotionally vulnerable. He gives us the ability to funnel overwhelming feelings to a separate compartment so we can continue to function externally. Once we're in a safer environment, God gives us the opportunity to process hidden feelings and memories.

Those who grew up in a home where parents were emotionally attentive and most of their developmental needs were met may have few, if any, compartments. But for folks who were emotionally neglected and/or abused, there may be multiple compartments spanning many developmental stages. Over the years, I've identified five main compartments that impact the ability to live an emotionally mature life: Guardian, Child, Teen, 20-something, Adult.

Guardian

Unfortunately, many children grow up in harmful environments that overwhelm them emotionally. It makes me really sad to hear stories where parents constantly told clients they were stupid or they would never amount to anything important. For many clients, sad/mad feelings were not allowed to be expressed at home. In other households, everyone was expected to tiptoe around an explosive parent, requiring disengagement from their own feelings. Many parents are emotionally unavailable, causing the child to be relationally immature. Emotionally needy parents drain everyone around them and neglect the legitimate needs of their children.

When ongoing emotional trauma threatens to crush us, an internal door closes on those emotions, allowing us to function in survival mode. The Guardian's sole function is to make sure you are protected. She/he looks at the world as something to be survived, like being in a bunker on the front line of a battle. Information about how to stay safe is gathered by watching and mimicking adults. The Guardian is hyper vigilant to any potential safety threat. She/he communicates through stabbing feelings of fear, anxiety, guilt, and self-condemnation, using these emotions to guide you to "safer" behaviors.

Jennifer called me recently asking if it was okay for her to take a day off work when she had flu symptoms and a temperature of 102 degrees. Asking what made her anxious about making that decision, Jennifer said she felt guilty for burdening other people at work without notice. Digging a little deeper, Jennifer realized she was actually worried her employer would fire her, even though she had plenty of vacation days available. This was her Guardian, afraid adult Jennifer was doing something wrong and she would get in trouble.

Because the Guardian part usually develops in early childhood, it operates out of a black and white view of the world. Young children are very literal and concrete. If you tell them you're running an errand, they expect you to put on your sneakers and jog out the door. They don't understand that people can be triggered in one context and take it out somewhere else. As a result, the Guardian's beliefs about how people interact and what is "right and wrong" are unnecessarily rigid.

Since the Guardian is usually the first part to develop, he/she is usually the strongest. Clients find the guilt feelings and being "in trouble" the hardest emotions to change. Most clients ask me how to get rid of the Guardian, but that would be getting rid of an important, valuable part of themselves. Instead, my hope is that the Guardian understands his/her protective role is no longer needed, recognizing he/she can contribute in a more positive, healthier way to the whole person.

I picture my Guardian as a little girl, about 5 years old, wearing grown up clothes. The dress and shoes are much too large for her, but she sees herself in that parental role, even though she's just a little girl. I know my Guardian tries to protect me out of caring and I love her for that, even when her overprotectiveness drives me crazy! These days when she gives me the "danger, danger" signal, I'm able to take a step back, give her a hug for the warning, but my Adult makes the decisions about what is true.

Child

Back in the 1970s, counselor and theologian John Bradshaw began speaking about the inner child hiding inside all of us. Although he took his theories a little too far at times, it was truly groundbreaking research. He linked relational deficits experienced in childhood to difficulties sustaining positive relationships in adulthood. Bradshaw said adults needed to experience supportive, non-shaming relationships in order for the wounded inner child to be healed.

Most of the time, the Child part contains the open, naive, trusting, caring qualities of our character. The Child laughs with abandon, loves fiercely, has that wonderful childlike innocence, and looks at life as an adventure. It's the Child who feels bad about leaving home in the morning to go to work because her kitty will be alone all day. When I watch a group of grown men making fun of each other's basketball skills, I suspect it's their inner Child come out to play.

Because children are naturally open and vulnerable, they don't know how to protect themselves emotionally, especially when wounds come from parents. When children are emotionally overwhelmed, the Guardian steps in to protect the Child. God created this automatic compartmentalization system to keep the most precious part of ourselves from being crushed. Once God leads us to a supportive, non-shaming, safe person, the Child compartment can open up and that part of us can be reclaimed.

For most of my clients, being able to experience God's loving kindness in me gives the Child the courage to open up and learn to be emotionally vulnerable. What an amazing, humbling opportunity I have every day to receive love from God, then to extend it to others in a way they can see and feel. The tangible expression of care in my office eventually allows clients to receive directly from God for themselves.

Teen

I absolutely love teenagers. They are full of energy, opinions, and attitudes. It's like they're being energized by the world. Talking to teens is like riding a roller coaster. Teen gals want to talk about everything relating to their life in the minutest detail. Who said what; what they wore; what they felt. Absolutely everything. Talking to teen guys is like waiting for water to boil on the stove. I ask a question, they stare at me, or the wall, or the floor for a while, then give me a one word answer.

Adolescence is a time for self-exploration. "Who am I and how do I relate to the world?" When parents don't allow mistakes and demand adherence to rules and expectations, teens can't develop their own identity. In an Outcome-based system, the high school years are seen as preparation for entry into adulthood. Teens are required to learn how to master adult values, adult behaviors, and how to play the adult game of climbing the corporate ladder. In God's Relational model, teens are encouraged to try all sorts of things on for size, seeing each item fits with who God made them to be. Giving teens the freedom to experiment with how they express their individuality allows them to develop a solid sense of self.

Unfortunately, most parents live out of fear. They want their child to be a happy, healthy, productive member of society, have a strong faith in God, and not make the same mistakes. While those are admirable hopes and dreams, the way most parents try to make that happen is to micro-manage their child's life, damaging the parent's relationship with their child and wounding occurs.

Learning to Make Decisions

When children are young, parents have almost complete control and strive to make perfect choices for their children. As the child grows, parents allow the child room to make their own decisions within a selection of "good" options. When a child begins to find their own individuality as a teen, parents need to allow room for "bad" choices. As Ben's parent, I will always step into my son's life if he's making catastrophic choices that will cause actual harm to himself or others. Giving him room, however, to make bad choices is one of the most difficult examples of sacrificial love. I don't want Ben to have his feelings hurt, lose money, fail a class, etc. I can foresee a lot of things he can't at his age. But to protect him from making mistakes prevents him from growing and maturing.

The Bible shows us many accounts of how God parented his earthly children. Take Sarah and Abraham, for instance. When God first told Sarah she would have a child, she laughed incredulously at the idea of conceiving a son at such an advanced age. Then she began to hope, talking and dreaming about it, waiting every month for the physical signs of pregnancy. Disappointment crept in and although she continued to give lip service to trusting in God, Sarah began to doubt.

Out of her disappointment, Sarah questioned God's heart and motives, choosing to take control back into her own hands. Like Eve, she misquoted God. Sarah told Abraham they must have misunderstood God, offering her maid Hagar to make up for God not keeping his promise.

What heartache this brought about to all involved. The tension between Sarah and Hagar was unbearable, even after the promised son, Isaac, was born. Abraham was caught in the middle of a situation he allowed to unfold because he didn't seek the Lord's blessing before sleeping with Hagar. Just wanting to keep the peace, he told Sarah to do whatever she thought best, turning a blind eye to Sarah's mistreatment. Hagar eventually fled into the desert with her son to escape Sarah's cruelty.

Most parents would have labeled Abraham and Sarah as incorrigible. We see several instances of how their immaturities got them into trouble. I don't see God shaking his finger at Sarah and Abraham for making bad choices, ruining his reputation, or for being obstinate. Instead, the New Testament lists Abraham as the Father of Israel, Friend of God, and Father of Faith. Sarah was chosen to carry a child who is part of the lineage of Jesus. How is it possible that folks who were so immature, made a lot of bad choices, did not trust God, caused pain and suffering to themselves and others can be held in such high esteem? Because God knew their potential and allowed them to grow and mature into their personhood through the process of making good and bad choices.

God's parenting shows us bad decisions are part of the learning process. Each time Abraham and Sarah failed, they learned more about themselves and God. Their bad decisions did impact others, but that's the price of learning how to love God, ourselves, and others well.

God was compassionate in caring for Hagar and Ishmael for the harm done to them in the midst of the process. In no way am I discounting the pain and misfortune Hagar and Ishmael suffered, nor the hurt you've suffered at the hands of another person. But there's no way to effectively work on process if we're tied up in knots about hurting those around us. Yes, we do need to care about the impact on others, but God calls us to have faith in His heart.

The Teen compartment holds all the anger, frustration, and despair at being denied the opportunity to live out personhood. The Teen is triggered when he/she feels like they're being shut down and their voice is being taken away.

Bobby grew up in a home where instant obedience without question was expected. His opinions were welcomed, so long as they perfectly mirrored those of his parents. Every time he gave a differing opinion, he was punished for being disrespectful. As a result, Bobby became tentative and fearful of making mistakes. At school, the other kids bullied him mercilessly. In college he was outwardly compliant, but one night his parents got a call saying Bobby was arrested for assault. When his father came to bail him out, Bobby was rude and arrogant, refusing to apologize or give an explanation. Everyone was shocked at his attitude and his actions.

Bobby began meeting with me to figure out what was going on inside. Sometimes he came into session with that same defiant attitude, other times he tearfully spent the entire session beating himself up. I explained the compartmentalization model to him and Bobby agreed his Guardian was scared because his Teen was trying to come to the surface and learn how to be a person. Because it was unsafe to show his personhood at home, Bobby locked up his Teen and functioned as expected. All the anger and aggression Bobby had stored up against dad came out when the Teen was triggered during the fight.

20-Something

Entering the adult world can be hugely intimidating. Competing for jobs with 40 year olds, buying your first car, signing your first lease, wondering if you really have anything to offer all cause anxiety. Every client in this age range has wavered between being excited to finish college and terrified they will crash and burn in the real world. Failing in life is much scarier than failing a class. I'm inspired to walk through this season with this age group. I find the idealism, creativity, and passion of the 20-Somethings refreshing.

Erikson says the goal of this stage of life is the ability to form relational commitments. When wounding has occurred, self-protective strategies keep us from connecting and bonding with others. The 20-Something compartment holds insecurities, self-doubt, longing to be validated, need to be seen as competent, and an increased longing for a stable, secure relationship. The 20-Something part is triggered when the person worries about figuring out and living life.

Beth was pushed into an adult parental role much too early in her childhood. Her mother was a nonfunctional alcoholic and dad demanded Beth keep the household running. By the age of 9, she made meals, did laundry, made sure her younger siblings took baths, and tucked them into bed. During her parents' screaming matches, Beth protectively hid the younger kids in a closet. While other 9 year olds went to birthday parties, played soccer, and snuggled with mom and dad, Beth pushed all her emotional needs into the Child compartment so she could survive. No one knew about the razor blades.

When Beth got into high school, her Teen part added drinking and meaningless hook-up sex to her other self-destructive behaviors. She made her escape from home as soon possible, determined to show her parents that someone else saw her as valuable. Beth worked her way through college and became a very successful, ruthless public defender. Each time she won a criminal case, Beth experienced a sense of power and satisfaction -- until she got home. Then the panic attack would start and all her insecurities came rushing to the surface.

Her 20-Something part compared her to other attorneys and other gals around her, always finding fault, convincing Beth she was a failure. Every relationship ended quickly and she felt her dreams of marriage and a family slip away. As she grieved for her lost Child, Beth was able to understand why she couldn't make relationships work. Today, Beth is reclaiming her enthusiasm and vision for living a joyful, meaningful life. She's learning how to be vulnerable and connect with others which brings her that needed sense of worth and value.

Adult

The Adult part encompasses the ability to problem-solve, see the big picture, handle conflict, and balance family and personal pressures. This part tends to be pragmatic, stable, and caring. All these qualities give the Adult the ability to re-parent the Child, Teen, and 20-Something. The Adult can learn how to validate, support, encourage, and love themselves. When all the parts learn to receive from the Adult and share their unique qualities, we're able to live out of the entire person God created us to be.

Coping Strategies

The ability to process difficult emotional situations and feelings is limited in childhood. God created an automatic shut-off valve that diverts these painful feelings into storage compartments. We utilize various coping strategies to lock the feelings and memories into rooms, allowing us to survive in the present. There are two main types of coping strategies: Avoidance and Resistance.

Avoidance

When a child cannot remove themselves from emotionally overwhelming people and environments, it's essential to develop avoidance survival skills.

- Avoidance of conflict
- Avoidance of feelings
- Avoidance of seeing truth about themselves and others
- Avoidance of acknowledging self-destructive behaviors

Avoidance can manifest several different ways; isolating, perfectionism, codependence, becoming the scapegoat, becoming ultra-responsible, etc. Developmentally, young children are egocentric, believing they have power, control, and influence over people and situations beyond themselves. Kids will strive to get all A's in school, play the peacemaker in the family, take the blame for making dad angry, etc. all in the hopes they can influence others to change so they can keep themselves safe. While the child continues to live at home, these "duck and cover" actions are necessary, but these strategies put kids at risk for repeating unhealthy patterns in their adult life. When these wounded adults eventually acknowledge they cannot make their life work, they end up in my office trying to understand what is wrong.

Resistance

Avoidance is about preservation. Deflection can be a way to preserve the precious little emotional energy one has by avoiding draining tasks or people. Preservation of our unique personhood is often a fulltime job.

Resistance is about fighting for your life. The resistant child knows in their gut what's going on at home is not okay and refuses to be muzzled. The more a parent tries to shut them up, the louder and more rebellious the child behaves. Denial of personhood is unacceptable because it feels like living dead. This child is hurt to their core by the emotional neglect and direct wounding by their parents, but it manifests differently. Hurt is shown by being disrespectful, lying, yelling, violence, self-harming, and attention seeking behaviors.

I actually believe it's healthier for children to fight for their personhood, even if it comes out sideways, than to allow themselves to become an empty shell. Rebelling is a necessary component of establishing personhood. What's tricky is giving Teens permission to push back in ways that don't result in long term or irreparable damage (i.e. dying hair purple vs. using heroin).

When parents call requesting counseling for their teenager, they often complain about rebellious behaviors and attitudes. Sometimes the parent wants me to help the child talk about their wounds, but most of the time they want me to push the kid back in line so they don't cause so much trouble for the family. Sorry parent, but I don't do it that way! (That's my Teen coming out!) I want my office to be a safe place where teenagers can express every emotion and share their pain without fear. It's my hope that when teens make a heart connection with me, they'll let their guard down and grow in personhood.

Become as a Little Child

Woundedness causes us to shut down, but the transformation process requires vulnerability and openness. No one is more vulnerable than a child. Choosing to be vulnerable feels unsafe and counterintuitive to most adults because of the hurt they've experienced as a child. Jesus' relationships with his heavenly father, earthly family, disciples, and friends were characterized by openness and a willingness for his heart to be seen. Vulnerability and transparency with safe, caring people are essential for wounds to be healed and our life to be transformed.

Every human being has a variety of needs; physical, emotional, social, intellectual, and spiritual. Although a newborn has all these needs, they have almost no ability to meet any of them. As a child grows older, needs become more complicated, but the ability to empower ourselves to meet some of the needs grows as well. There will, however, always be some level of gap. God's plan to address this gap is to facilitate meeting needs primarily through other people. Sometimes God intervenes directly himself, but most of the time needs are met by living a "one another" relational lifestyle.

I see this principle in Matthew 11 when Jesus explains we need to become like little children. Kids understand and accept dependence, so they aren't shy about freely sharing wants and needs. Kids will volunteer all sorts of information about what they like, what they don't, how it's unfair their brother got the bigger piece of cake, and every overheard comment their parents don't want shared with the world! When Jesus told the disciples they needed to be like a little child to enter the Kingdom of God, he was talking about vulnerability; approaching life with openness. As you sit on the couch across from me, I can hear you take a deep breath and look at me like I'm crazy.

> "So, let me get this straight," you say as if speaking to a deranged person. "God created us with core longings and a set of complicated needs that are supposed to get met by others when I'm in my most vulnerable state?"

> "Yes," I reply.

> "But what happens when that person not only doesn't meet my needs, but seriously hurts me because I'm so open?"

> "Do you choose to never drive your car again because you had a car accident in the past? No, you continue driving and develop a healthy discernment about the vehicles around you. Living a hopeful, faith-based life is about risk. You can choose to let fear dictate your quality of life or you can learn how to be good at processing disappointment and hurt on the way to joy and meaningfulness."

It's my heartfelt prayer that you talk to God about your desire for true healing of your wounds rather than continuing to use denial and fear to lock them away. You can learn how to let go of the old self-protective strategies and learn how to keep yourself from harm. God helps children develop survival strategies to protect their heart, soul,

'. While those strategies are essential in childhood,
lult's ability to have healthy, loving relationships. The
;od will give us discernment as to the character of oth-
.nd their ability to be positive or negative in our life.

Vulnerability and Transparency

The Bible clearly tells us God wants us to experience an abundant,
full, prospering life, even in this broken, troubled world. That can
only come about when we understand loving well is the key and put
all our energy into identifying and pushing through the barriers. The
abundant life encompasses love, joy, peace, patience, kindness, goodness, faithfulness, gentleness, and self-control. There's no way we can
achieve any of these fruits without a vulnerable and transparent heart.

Many Christians find it shameful to admit it feels unsafe to trust
those parts of us that are most precious with anyone, even God. One
of the hardest parts of the healing process is tolerating that horrible
exposed feeling while trying to connect with what is true. Being able
to trust God's motives and receive love from Him cannot take place
without the uncomfortableness of feeling weak and vulnerable.

In William Young's book, *The Shack*, each member of the trinity
pursues the main character, Mack. Their intimate, probing questions
shine a light on his deeply buried thoughts, beliefs, and feelings. Like
most of us, Mack is caught off guard by God's ability to look past the
surface and he feels acutely uncomfortable at his transparency. When
Adam and Eve were in relationship with God in the Garden, they
lived an open, vulnerable lifestyle. The decision to protect themselves
introduced fear. It's at that point the Bible tells us they saw their na-
kedness and were ashamed.

I imagine this was what Judas experienced at the last supper when
Jesus said someone there would betray him. Jesus didn't mention Judas by name, but I'm certain Judas felt like there was a huge spotlight

from heaven showing the darkness in his heart. Jesus loved Judas dearly and was giving him an opportunity to confess his heart attitude. But Judas was not able to tolerate his own guilt at being exposed. Rather than clearly seeing Jesus' loving motives and responding to his loving kindness, Judas ran away from what Jesus offered and betrayed him. The weight of seeing his own cowardice and inability to receive Jesus' love sadly brought Judas to despair and he chose death.

I'm humbled by the courage of new clients to make the choice to open up and talk about deeply painful issues with a stranger. They come in nervous, not sure what I will ask of them or whether I have anything of value to give. Even clients who've come in every week for a year find it hard at times to be vulnerable when they feel shame. People are made to bond and attach to others by way of our feelings. We then generalize what we learn from those relationships.

If we experience our father as strict and detached, we'll usually see God that same way. When we've bonded with someone and they hurt us at a deep level, scar tissue forms that hinders our ability to form a bond with someone else. That's why the therapeutic relationship is so important. In order for clients to remove the scar tissue in their relationships, they need to re-learn how to do relationship with a safe, caring person who does it well. Once clients have made progress in their Roadmap to Freedom journey, they'll be able to apply the same principles to their relationship with God and others.

Healing Wounds

No matter who wounded you, how many compartments you possess, or what coping mechanisms you've used, there is hope for healing and transformation. God allows our woundedness to come to the surface when we're able to do the work to gain freedom. This process has four stages: Processing Emotions, Critiquing Beliefs, Truthful Confession, and Living Free. It's my prayer that you will find the courage to take this healing journey as we walk through these stages in the following chapters.

REFLECTION QUESTIONS

1. What are some ways you've been wounded?

2. How do you feel when you consider that your parents failed to love you perfectly?

3. Which Negative Resolution wounds do you see in your life?

4. Do you see evidence of emotional compartments?

5. Which compartment interferes most with living a healthy adult life?

6. In what ways does your fear-based belief system impact your ability to follow God's leading and enjoy life?

7. How big was your backyard?

8. Which type of coping strategy do you primarily utilize?

9. In what ways has God called you to become more like a little child?

10. What fears do you have about allowing yourself to be vulnerable?

CHAPTER 6

Processing Emotions

Why does God create us with messy, complicated feelings? How frustrating is it when the head and the heart are not in sync? We try to arm wrestle our emotions into agreement with our belief system by telling ourselves or others, *"Stop worrying about that," "You're making a mountain out of a molehill,"* or *"It's not that big of a deal."* When those admonitions don't work, we usually resort to condemnation. *"You're just a drama queen," "I must not be good enough,"* or *"Stop being so sensitive."*

Many clients tell me their goal is to cut feelings out of their life. This makes sense if you've chosen to live an Outcome-based lifestyle. Pushing the feelings into the emotional holding tank does allow you to be more dependable, responsible, accountable, and all the other qualities prioritized in that world view. It reminds me of the *Incredible Hulk* TV show. Dr. Banner turns into a huge, scary, green monster when he becomes emotionally overwhelmed. The Hulk destroys things and causes mayhem, but he also rescues people and delivers justice to wrongdoers. Dr. Banner's goal was to find a cure so he could live a quiet, peaceful, controlled life. In my view, the Hulk is formed out of all the emotions Dr. Banner failed to process. While Dr. Banner was educated, intelligent, and focused on his work, the Hulk embodied his most important, interesting, and unique qualities! I'd love to invite both Dr. Banner and the Hulk to sit on my couch and talk about

how they can bring their strengths together to live an integrated, empowered life. Or we could just talk about what it's like to be huge and
green!

Truth is, our ability to be moved emotionally is another area
where we're made in the image of a relational God. Compartmentalization happens because our capacity for feeling complicated emotions
is in place before we can intellectually process and interpret their
meaning. It's impossible to have healthy relationships and love ourselves and others well without experiencing feelings. While emotions
do not equal truth, they do give us valuable information as to who
God made us to be based on how we experience the world.

Permission

No earthly parent can meet all their child's emotional needs. There
are personality differences, gender differences, different priorities,
immaturities, and different preferences. When parents don't understand, cannot, or choose not to meet their child's needs, kids are sad,
disappointed, and angry. Children need help processing the feelings
rather than chastised for how the feelings manifest.

God provides a safety valve to funnel emotions into a holding tank
when life isn't emotionally safe. While this process allows you to protect yourself, it also creates a barrier between you and others. You've
learned how to guard your heart, but your ability to receive from God
and others has been compromised. It's like God built you an inner fortress with no drawbridge. Even when clients acknowledge how their
self-protectedness keeps them in prison and agree vulnerability and
transparency are necessary, they still don't know how to let their
guard down.

Change begins with permission -- believing you have permission
to experience and share your feelings openly. Embracing this right is

like standing on the top of Mt. Everest. The exhilaration clients feel when given permission to view the world through their own experience is awe inspiring. Were you were told directly not to have feelings or given indirect messages that others were uncomfortable with your emotions? Permission creates a drawbridge to the tank holding past wounds while allowing you to process feelings differently in the present.

For some clients, it takes months or longer to become comfortable with acknowledging and experiencing their true feelings. They've trained themselves to take cues from others as to what they "should" think and feel. Kind of like Julia Roberts in *Runaway Bride*. Her character had literally run away from three different grooms during three different wedding ceremonies. A news reporter was sent to do a story about the bride. He interviewed all three men asking the question, "How does she like her eggs?" Each one answered, "Same as me."

As the reporter observed the bride interacting with family and friends, he observed she wasn't living her own life, but became a chameleon to please others. When the bride finally saw the fortress she had built, she decided to focus on learning who she was, what she felt, and how she liked her eggs. Several months later, the runaway bride sought out the reporter to report she preferred eggs benedict. Giving herself permission to emotionally experience her own life allowed the bride to eventually enter into marriage as a whole person.

Information and Energy

Feelings give us two important things necessary for transformation: Information and Energy. Emotional information is critical in being able to live a relational lifestyle. Empathy, compassion, and sacrificial love are all fueled by our ability to be emotionally vulnerable. When we're standing on the emotional river bank watching other people struggle with waves of feeling, our heart is not engaged. We shout out directions or vent our frustration with their process, but they cannot receive from us.

If we're sitting in the other person's boat, we become overwhelmed with their feelings and codependently take on their burdens. A healthy lifestyle is where we navigate our own boat through the river of life with God as our Captain, allowing others to pull alongside us with encouragement, and empathetically supporting others ourselves.

When feelings are shut off or dismissed, we miss out on valuable information God uses to reveal personhood. We're not created as "one size fits all" people. Just as God created multiple varieties of birds, animals, and plants, He created each of us as unique and special. Wanting to feel special is one of the core longings God instilled in our soul. When this message isn't communicated from our parents, we shut down our feelings and often go into victim-mode. Owning our feelings allows God to show us how we respond to the world in our own, unique way. Knowing what shuts me down emotionally allows me to protect myself in a healthy way from harmful people and situations.

Clients ask me how to clearly hear from God, wanting to know how to discern God's plan for their life. There's no way to establish walkie talkie communication with God without being an excellent student of our emotions. Feelings allow God to communicate through the Holy Spirit to our soul. I spend a lot of time with God discussing how I experience people. Every time I talk with a new client, I'm trying to open myself up to how I feel in their presence, what they say, what they talk about, and what God shows me about their heart attitude. I ask the Holy Spirit to sort through all my thoughts and feelings and give me insight into the client's character and discernment about whether we will be a good fit for each other. I get a red light/green light sense in my gut that I've learned is God speaking to me.

Learning to correctly interpret our emotions is a trial and error process. Most of us are much more comfortable living in fear, relying on black and white facts to make sure we are "right." Giving up the illusion of certainty is brutal. It feels like God is asking us to jump off a cliff without knowing how far we will fall.

Trust in the transformation process gives you courage. Most of us desperately cling to certainty for safety, but living free is about risk. I began stepping out in small ways to find out if I could trust my gut. When I got a red light feeling about a person, I asked more questions and watched their life for a while. It really did became clear what God was communicating to me. I became bolder, asking people if they had certain thoughts or felt a particular way, and usually they agreed with my discernment. When I missed the mark, I learned it wasn't a fatal, catastrophic failure but a learning experience.

Emotions also give us energy to overcome fear. In some households, anger was used to overpower, intimidate, and harm. But emotions can be used positively to push through fear barriers. I've read amazing accounts where adrenaline provided people the physical strength and courage to act in a crisis. King David was the only one able to harness his outrage and use it to step out on the battlefield and challenge Goliath.

When I need to have a difficult conversation, I first squeeze out all the worry and fear. Venting all my knee-jerk self-protective defenses allows me to anchor to what God has shown me is true. John 8:32 says that God's truth will set us free. I now know what freedom feels like, so I can use that knowledge to give me the needed boost to enter into that scary conversation with courage and confidence.

It's amazing to me how Jesus stayed open emotionally while in the midst of relationships with immature human beings. He experienced sadness, hurt, pain, and disappointment in his parents and siblings just like every other human being. Many times, we see Jesus' frustration with the disciples over their lack of understanding, inability to trust God, and immature selfishness. Instead of shutting down and detaching from the messiness of this world, Jesus embraced the opportunity to fully experience life as a vulnerable, emotional human being.

Garden of Gethsemane

We can read numerous accounts in both the Old Testament and New Testament where God and Jesus exhibited a wide range of emotions. Studying biblical accounts of God's emotions helps us understand and use our own feelings in a positive, loving way. Minimizing the role of emotions means missing out on information and energy. If we live solely out of emotion and always equate it to truth, then we don't have a firm, godly foundation.

Living free means learning the balance between living smart and goal oriented recklessly.

I had the amazing opportunity to visit Israel a few years ago. It was surreal driving down a rocky road passing a Palestinian settlement on the left, a heavily protected Israeli settlement on the right, and seeing road signs for Jericho ahead. Coming from suburban Columbus, Ohio, it was very disconcerting to see such an obvious military presence everywhere I went. Each time I left the West Bank, I had to stop at a checkpoint for questioning. On one occasion, soldiers insisted I go through an X-ray screening procedure similar to those found at airports. I was told to vacate the vehicle so it could be inspected. The soldiers opened all the van doors to do a thorough search and even led bomb-sniffing dogs around the vehicle. I was certainly not in Kansas anymore Toto!

I went swimming in the Mediterranean Sea near Tel-Aviv next to Roman aqueduct ruins. Bobbing up and down like an apple in the Dead Sea, I slathered myself with the mineral-rich black mud people in New York City pay thousands of dollars to import. I took a boat ride on the Sea of Galilee and enjoyed watching youngsters demonstrate Jewish celebration dances and sing worship songs in Hebrew. As I took a photo of my feet in the Jordan River, folks on white water rafts floated past me! Nearby were several Palestinian women in full veils watching their naked toddlers play in the water. I visited the town of Capernaum, touched ancient olive presses, and gazed in wonder at the ruins historians claim is the site of the Apostle Peter's house.

Standing on top of a hill overlooking Samaria, I felt the presence of God and sensed the sandaled feet that had passed this way. Psalm 121:1 came to mind. *"I lift up my eyes to the hills--where does my help come from? My help comes from the Lord, the Maker of heaven and earth." (NIV)* What an amazing opportunity to lay my eyes on the same mountains that prompted David's praise to the Lord.

It was awe-inspiring to stand in the center of the Old City, looking at the Wailing Wall to my right and the Temple Mount's golden dome to my left. We spent an afternoon walking through Hezekiah's tunnel. In 2 Chronicles 32, it tells us how King Hezekiah commissioned an underground water aqueduct built to bring water into the walled city of Jerusalem. He was expecting an assault by the Assyrians and the city did not have a water source. One digging team started at the Pool of Siloam and the other went a third of a mile away to the Spring of Gibhon, tunneling toward Jerusalem. It was an astounding engineering feat to line up the two excavations to deliver the water from the spring into the city.

Viewing the City of Jerusalem from the Mount of Olives, I had a profound sense of living in the past, present, and future all at the same time. According to Zephaniah 14:4, resurrection of the dead begins when the Messiah sets foot on the Mount of Olives. The entire Kidron valley between the Mount of Olives and the City of Jerusalem was a sea of white stone burial boxes dating back to antiquity.

The account of Jesus in the Garden of Gethsemane shows the genuineness of living an emotionally open life. Being able to actually see the ancient, gnarled olive trees surrounded by white stone allowed me to capture the feeling of what it was like for Jesus that night. He'd been telling the disciples for weeks that going to Jerusalem would bring about his death. Talking about it was preparing both the disciples and Jesus for the upcoming events. Jesus knew he was going to not only experience a great deal of cruelty and physical pain, but also overwhelming emotional and relational sorrow.

As Jesus was praying, he began to be sorrowful and troubled, sharing those feelings with Peter, James, and John. (Matthew 26) Jesus was so burdened with the enormity of the task that lay ahead of him, he asked the disciples to stay awake and pray for him to be strengthened. He was asking them to mourn with him as he mourned. Jesus could have asked God to send a host of angels to care for him, but angels are not made in God's image and couldn't join with Jesus in a deep, emotional way.

I'm most struck by Jesus' humanity. The Bible reports his deep emotional state caused him to fall to his knees, his face to the ground. Jesus honestly, fervently begged God to find a way to take the cup from him. This God-man Jesus was in agony knowing what excruciating pain he would suffer and he did the human thing of asking God if there was a Plan B. Without this picture of Christ in his humanness, I would forever feel like a coward when I ask God to take away the hardships in my life.

Jesus honestly and genuinely allowed himself to feel all the emotions surrounding his impending death. He wasn't ashamed to be vulnerable and transparent in front of the disciples and God. I love that

Jesus didn't use some sort of rationalization or minimization of his feelings. He didn't sound like a pompous martyr, saying he knew it would be hard, but he would clench his teeth and march through it. No, he wept.

At some later point, Jesus returned to the disciples and found them sleeping, exhausted from sorrow. Jesus woke them, encouraging them to pray so they would not fall into temptation. I disagree with opinions that villainize the disciples, saying they were lazy or didn't really care about Jesus' concerns. The text says they were exhausted from sorrow. Have you ever grieved and cried so deeply that you were exhausted? Then you know this type of mourning comes from the bottom of your soul because someone you love is hurting. Jesus' words were said to put them on high alert because he knew his arrest was imminent.

We are uniquely vulnerable to the discouraging voice of the enemy in the midst of a heart-wrenching season. The enemy can be found in words spoken by hurtful people when we need compassion or in our own condemning words about what we should have said or done. But almost always, the enemy takes on the form of the serpent in the Garden of Eden, making us question whether God really loves us. The disciples would soon be surrounded by this enemy.

Three times Jesus begged the disciples to stay alert and pray because temptation was upon them. But for all their good intentions, Matthew tells us their bodies were weak. Next thing they know, a large armed crowd shows up and arrests Jesus. Bedlam breaks loose as Peter grabs his sword and starts swinging it around in panic, threatening everybody, even cutting off someone's ear. We then hear the strong, confident, powerful voice of Jesus call out to Peter. The same voice that calmed the storm on the Sea of Galilee restored order to the Garden of Gethsemane.

Jesus reminded Peter he didn't need Peter's protection. He had the power to ask his Father in heaven to send down legions of angels. Jesus also reminded the crowd he had made himself available in the temple courts every day, so their armed show of strength now was obviously unnecessary. In fact, Jesus declared he had known all along he was the fulfillment of the writings of the prophets. By his words, Jesus gave notice he stood ready to take on all the pain and suffering those next days would bring.

So how did Jesus go from weeping in the garden to exhibiting strength and determination in the moment of his arrest? He had poured out his heart and emotions in prayer to his Father. In return, God sent an angel to give him strength when the disciples had none to give Jesus. Every week I have folks weeping in my office, pouring out their hurt and disappointment. Most of the time they know I don't have any answers to change their circumstances. They walk out my door and nothing is fixed. Yet their burden's been lifted, allowing them to continue to persevere. When we're given the gift of someone praying and waiting with us in that emotional time, we receive comfort which comes directly from God's heart. Knowing in our soul that God sees us in that difficult place, that His heart hurts with us, and that he is bringing joy out of ashes allows us to press forward with determination.

Fixing Feelings

I get really frustrated with the church because it generally does such a poor job of teaching people to love the brokenhearted. I grew up in church and I've attended an assortment of different denominations. I've got a lot of experience in this arena. I've read countless Christian self-help books, attended lots of conferences, been a part of and led tons of bible studies, and attended seminary. I've heard many admonitions about loving your neighbor and sermons on how to live out the beatitudes, etc. But most people, including pastors, feel uncomfortable and awkward around someone who's an emotional mess. It's much easier to problem solve, step in and fix something, or give bumper sticker platitudes. I think that's because most people are uncomfortable with their own feelings. This is where maturity vs. codependence shows itself. When we're comfortable with our own feelings, we can listen to someone else without the need to fix it for them or for ourselves.

Many times, people are uncomfortable with how they feel about someone else's situation, wanting everything to be all fine quickly so no one feels "bad." Instead, I believe the church should help folks value the ability to sit in sorrow with others. Isaiah talks about the Messiah as being a man of sorrows, acquainted with grief. Learning to be comfortable sitting in those deep, dark places with each other is mandatory in order to love well. Look at the account of the death and resurrection of Lazarus in John 11.

When Jesus received word Lazarus was sick, God told Jesus the sickness would not end in death. He said this event would be an opportunity to show Jesus' divinity. The account doesn't record that Jesus sent any type of message back to Mary and Martha. They must have been frantic, wondering what would keep Jesus away from the man whom he loved so much.

When the disciples heard they were returning to Judea, they reminded Jesus he'd just left because he was in danger of being stoned. The disciples were completely confused, wondering why Jesus would put them all in danger to wake up a sleeping man. (John was definitely not afraid to reveal both the positives and negatives about the disciples in his gospel. The disciples were always misunderstanding Jesus. Of course, it's not quite as funny when I'm the dumb one!)

The journey to Bethany must have taken quite some time because when they arrived, Lazarus had been in the tomb for four days. I find it interesting to see how different people responded differently to Jesus' arrival. There were a number of mourners who judged Jesus, grumbling that he should have gotten himself there earlier so he could have healed Lazarus. When word came to Mary and Martha that Jesus was near, Martha immediately went to him, but Mary stayed at home.

Luke gives us some insight on Mary and Martha's personalities. In Luke 10, he writes that at an earlier visit, Mary sat at Jesus' feet when he visited and Martha was distracted by preparations for her guests. When Martha complains to Jesus, he lovingly, but firmly, explains the difference between a task-based way of life and a relational one. I can see Jesus standing in the kitchen, looking at all the food Martha is preparing. He talks about loving her heart of service and how he's looking forward to enjoying her cooking. But Jesus also reminds Martha that the good work of her hands is temporary and she needs to see that being in relationship is God's first priority.

Now fast forward to John 11 and Martha is the first one to run to Jesus as he arrives after Lazarus' death. She tells him she knows he would have healed Lazarus if he had been there. Martha declares that she knows God will give Jesus whatever he asks, even raising someone from the dead four days later. To me, her words show her growth from their previous conversation. Some people hear a judgmental, condemning tone, but I think she was acknowledging all the relationships involved; Jesus loves Lazarus, God loves Jesus, and through knowing Jesus, we can know God. As Martha changed her paradigm to viewing life through a relational lens, she was able to embrace Jesus in the midst of this difficult time.

Because of Martha's trust in him, Jesus shares with her the truth - that he is the Messiah and those who believe in him will never die. I think I would've been on emotional overload at this point. My brother's just died and even though I trusted in Jesus' reasons to not come in time to heal him, I would've still been sad. Now, Jesus is telling me he's the long awaited Messiah and has come to bring everlasting life! I don't know what I would have done with all those feelings and all that information. What Martha did was to embrace the truth Jesus shared, acknowledge her understanding of what it meant, and then run to bring her sister to Jesus.

Grieving

John tells us Jesus was deeply moved by the tears and sadness of Lazarus' family and friends to the point that he sat down with them and wept. It's a profoundly exquisite picture. Jesus allowing himself to experience their grief. His heart felt it so deeply that he was transparent with his own feelings. To me, this is even more beautiful in light of the fact that he knew he was there to raise Lazarus from the dead.

Grieving the failures of our parents, hurtful actions of others, and the destructive consequences of our own choices is cleansing. It means recognizing those hurts, valuing their impact, understanding our unhealthy responses, giving ourselves the grace and mercy God gives us, and coming to acceptance.

Grieving begins with allowing ourselves to feel.

What I see in the church is an emphasis on shutting down emotions and slapping a bumper sticker slogan on our forehead. We've all heard, and maybe said, platitudes such as, *"All things work together for good," "He/she's in a better place," "God won't give you any more than you can handle,"* or *"This will help you grow closer to God."* I get so frustrated with these types of statements because the speaker's motive is usually to get the listener to disengage from what they are feeling. When we say these things, it gives the message that anything other than being peaceful and feeling blessed is unbiblical. No, no, no and NO!

When we live an interdependent "one another" lifestyle, we SHOULD have lots of feelings as we go through our day. Feelings are like the check engine light in your car. They lead you to open the hood and locate the source. Feelings come out of beliefs, so asking ourselves why something affects us emotionally uncovers beliefs we can then discuss with God. One of the most damaging beliefs taught in the church is to discount and minimize feelings. Doing so causes us to completely bypass the God-ordained opportunity to uncover and critique beliefs that may have been installed incorrectly.

When I get to heaven, I can't wait to have a conversation with Mary and ask why she waited to go to Jesus. Had she been grieving so deeply that she had little strength or was she trying to process her disappointment with Jesus for not arriving sooner? She was the one who had sat at his feet, absorbing every word, forging a strong, emotional bond. It makes sense she may have been confused and deeply hurt, not understanding how Jesus could let such a terrible thing happen to her brother. I think most human beings have, at some point in their life, asked this same question of God. I've learned that trying to reconcile painful, tragic circumstances on earth with God's claims of loving us is impossible in a human created outcome-based system. It can only be understood within the framework of relationship.

Jesus could have arrived in Bethany with shouts of celebration that he was there to fix everything and make it all better. But he didn't. He allowed himself to be moved by the pain of death in this world and its effect on humanity. Death was not part of God's original plan for us. For Jesus to feel its impact on humankind shows us the depth of his love and respect for our pain.

God's Timing

God has created so many amazing automatic processes in our body. We breathe without thinking about it, our muscles move when we decide to do something, our growling stomachs are very good at keeping time, and babies independently decide when they're ready to be born! God's timing in the healing process is also unique to each person. Moving forward towards difficult feelings and memories needs to be at the pace of the client. Some clients may need to tell the same stories over and over again until they can reconnect memories to emotions. Viewing progress from an outcome-based lens, we can mistakenly believe we're stuck or going backwards. When a client thinks they're just going 'round and 'round the same mulberry bush, oftentimes they are connecting emotionally at a deeper level.

Janae recently confessed she stopped journaling because she keeps writing the same facts about the same events and she still feels numb. I told her to look at it as needing to prime a rusty old hand-crank water pump. It would be helpful if we could just turn on the feelings water fountain, but most of us have been avoiding our feelings for years. It takes time and intentionality to open them up again. When you spend time writing and talking about the same events, you may be strengthening your resolve to feel and value your emotions in a healthier way. Oil rig crews dig for oil, sometimes for weeks or months, but when they hit the pocket of oil, it's a gusher. Same with emotions. It can be scary and overwhelming, so being prepared and taking your time makes sense.

As feelings begin to flow, it's important to learn how to float downstream rather than analyze. Our knee-jerk response to feelings is usually to try and figure something out or take some sort of action. We need to put on our water wings and let the current carry us along, trusting in the process.

I'm very honored by the trust my clients show in allowing them-selves to be vulnerable with their emotions in my presence. This is precisely how they've been hurt in the past, by other people taking advantage of their vulnerability. For them to choose not to self-pro-tect and trust I'm guiding them to a godly, healthy place is how they begin to rebuild trust in God.

Learning how to tolerate feelings is essential to cleaning out the emotional holding tank. I believe many people self-anesthetize with addictive behaviors because they haven't learned this skill. Twelve-step groups are important in helping people focus on changing atti-tudes and behaviors related to addictions, but it's also important to work on the pain and hurt at the root of the avoidant behaviors. The folks who seem to have the hardest time with this step are those who suffer from anxiety.

> Anxiety takes the place of true feelings and becomes a barrier to looking inside the holding tank.

Anxiety about what kind of person I am. Worry I'm not as good of a person as I want to be. Concern that if I acknowledge what I really feel, it'll change my relationships, etc. When we focus on worry and anxiety, it distracts us from hard feelings that need processing.

A couple years ago I was looking at my checking account online and I didn't see evidence that a payment had gone out to pay my son's credit card bill. (Yes, I'm very blessed to be able to help my son out financially while he's in college.) My bank had changed its bill pay sys-tem a couple months earlier. I immediately jumped to the conclusion that I'd completely messed up my son's credit by not paying on his credit card. My anxiety began to rise, causing me to focus on all the negative "what if" worries, convincing me I'd ruined Ben financially for life. Concerned he'd be angry with me, I felt like a horrible mother.

The underlying belief was that I'm responsible to take every precaution available to protect my child from every harm. If I feel like I've failed, I equated it to a character issue, not just a mistake.

Heart beating out of my chest, I wanted to jump off the roof to get rid of all the nervous worry energy. I texted Ben to ask him to check his credit card account, but I knew he probably wouldn't get back to me for several hours. At that point I had a decision to make. Do I sit in the feelings and wait for the anxiety to come down so I could find out what's true? Or do I use my old self-protective pattern of trying to feel better by nagging Ben, calling the bank, wringing my hands, and telling everyone what a bad mother I was, etc.? Having been down this road many times, I knew if I waited out the anxiety, I'd be able to get more clarity.

I took a walk around the office to shake off the tension and did a bunch of self-talk, reminding myself I wanted to handle this in a healthy way. These steps allowed me to set the anxiety aside and I was able to focus in on caring for my scheduled clients. A few hours later I was feeling calmer and believed all the things I had told myself were true. I could now believe I'd never intentionally hurt my son in any way. Ben might be frustrated at the situation, but it wouldn't change our relationship.

Underneath my anxiety was sadness. This incident reminded me that being human means I can't always keep my son safe. Taking a deep breath, I again pulled up the bank account and guess what? Yup, the payment was there in black and white, I'd just skipped over it. Whew! I hung in, tolerated the anxiety and negative messaging, uncovered what I was actually feeling, and corrected the mistaken messages.

Eventually the feelings current slows down and we begin to talk about context. Without context, we won't have all the puzzle pieces to get clarity about events and our role. You've probably tried to reassure someone they weren't at fault about a circumstance. Although they could agree with you intellectually, they probably still felt guilt or shame. We need to allow the feelings to come to the surface first before we can stand back from the situation to see everything and come to an emotional resolution.

Once our well of feelings begins to flow through journaling, talking, and experiencing life, we then look for the beliefs that are uncovered when we're emotionally triggered.

Beliefs that have not been critiqued often sound like *shoulds, shouldn'ts, have tos, always, nevers, "I have no other choice," or "I feel like a bad___."* Accompanying emotions are hopelessness, anxiety, despair, and feeling stuck.

I don't see anywhere in the Bible where these feelings are associated with God. So to me, it's a good bet the beliefs associated with these emotions need to be reviewed. Learning how to submit these beliefs to God and to directly hear from Him about what is true is a step many of us miss. In our limited understanding, we can't see how there could be an answer other than the one we believe, so we sit in a black hole of despair. In the next chapter, I talk about how to uncover and examine your beliefs in the presence of God.

REFLECTION QUESTIONS

1. How did your family view the role of feelings?

2. Do you give yourself and others permission to have and express feelings?

3. In what ways do you shut off your emotions?

4. Do you feel weak and vulnerable when you allow others to see your emotions?

5. Are you uncomfortable when others are openly emotional?

6. What steps do you take to "fix" feelings?

7.   How do you respond to God in times of pain and hurt?

8.   What is the purpose of grieving?

9.   What fears do you have about allowing your feelings to come to the surface?

10.   What benefit do you see in learning to process emotions?

The Waves of Victory

A few ripples kiss my toes, then recede. Inexorably, the sea continues to advance; unrelenting in its determination to claim that which is its own. Unremitting in its persistence, unyielding in its force, I am captivated. The riptide draws the waves back, and the sand under my feet is washed away. The receding water exposes a firm foundation which cannot be eroded. Choosing not to resist the compelling current that surrounds me, I surrender to Him who is mightier than I.

In the same way the waves are pulled back to their source, God patiently, but persistently, draws us closer to Himself. Because He loves us dearly, He will not allow us to remain rooted in our sin, but longs to immerse us in his Awesome Greatness. He continuously woos us, wave after wave, through his love, mercy, and convicting Spirit. By responding to his call, we choose to yield to His Lordship, and are swallowed up in His Grace.

CHAPTER 7

Critiquing Beliefs
?

I'm in the middle of a knockdown, drag out, name-calling feud! As part of my office manager role, I've chosen to take on maintenance of the office equipment. Today I'm having a tug-of-war with our fax machine. I'm the one who bought it, so I brought the fight on myself.

Yesterday I saw the dreaded message that the fax was out of ink. Knowing this would be a showdown at the O-K corral, I waited until today to roll up my sleeves and get my hands dirty. I chose to buy the kind of fax machine that uses carbon copy printer rolls because it's cheaper than ink cartridges. We don't send/receive that many faxes, so I thought it would be more cost effective. But every three months or so, I have to gather up the patience to wrestle with those black printer rolls in plastic holders. Now I could make it easy on myself and buy the printer rolls already installed in the holders, but they cost a lot more than just buying the replacements. Problem is, my brain doesn't process mechanical drawing type instructions, so I have to re-learn what goes where and what direction it all faces every single time.

The first time I changed the printer roll, I was so fed up with the process that I grabbed my keys, drove to Staples, and bought the prepared one just to use as an illustrative model. Looking at that model today, I think the blue knob goes on the back left side and the black knob sits on the front right side, the large carbon roll side goes in the back and the yellow one fits in the front. Or is it the other way around? Even when I get it set-up correctly, installing the holder in the machine can be a nightmare. I always have to re-insert the holder at least a dozen times before it pulls the carbon correctly and print actually appears on the page.

This is an epic battle to watch. I'm not a competitive person and here I'm making threatening comments to an inanimate object, feeling like we are locked together in a wrestling death match! I finally get the carbon roll in the holder. But when I eventually get the holder in the fax, the machine eats not only the black page, but pulls a sheet of paper in with it, making loud crunching noises. Here I come in early to get the task accomplished and when my first client of the day arrives, it's still messed up. At this point I give up and put the expensive holder in the machine!

While in the midst of this debacle, Mark walks in and starts to greet me. I shake my finger at him, saying I'm in a horrible mood because I'm dealing with the *&^%^ fax machine. He definitely knows what that means! As I struggle, he quietly offers to buy a new fax machine, one that's much easier to service. Immediately I decline his offer because my stubbornness will not yet allow me to admit defeat.

So what do I learn about myself from this incident? It shows me that I continue to live out of old tapes saying I'm incompetent, that my inability to make life work smoothly shows a lack of personal value and worth. As long as this message is triggered by people or events, I can't let go of my own Plan A and receive support from others. The beliefs we have about ourselves, God, and others have a profound effect on what we think, feel, and do. I always use the analogy of making pasta to explain this concept. Water is essential in the cooking process, but you need to drain the liquid to uncover the pasta. Venting feelings freely allows beliefs to be revealed and critiqued.

Beliefs are the glasses through which we interpret the world and everything that happens.

Two people can attend the same event and have completely different experiences based on the glasses they wear. Beliefs lead to thoughts; thoughts lead to feelings; and feelings cause us to either move forward or away in response. When my clients tell me they want to stop feeling terrible, I recommend we look at the root belief that is telling them something is wrong to see if that belief is true. It's both scary and exhilarating to embrace permission to wrestle through beliefs with God versus accepting confinement by someone else's interpretations of right and wrong.

Beliefs About Ourselves

Writing this book has been one of the most challenging, yet rewarding tasks I have ever accomplished. I've been amazed at the fears that have emerged. Negative voices from my past have resurfaced. I've had anxieties about showing vulnerability, concern for how my concepts will be received by unknown readers, and some fears that are just ordinary, human writer insecurities. Observing what those fears are, where they came from, and how I respond to them have led to many conversations with God, family, friends, and clients. I live my life in a fishbowl, believing by sharing my process, it will inspire and encourage others to do process themselves.

Beliefs about ourselves are usually intermixed with truth. I often ask clients to write a list of their positive and negative character qualities. The items on the lists themselves are interesting, but I'm much more fascinated by WHY they list it as good or bad. For instance, Susan listed being too emotional as a negative trait. When I asked why she viewed it as negative, Susan related how her engineer dad was always telling her not to bring emotions into the decision-making process. Her belief was founded on the way someone else lived their life, not on how God created her to live. She never even considered that approaching life through an emotional lens could actually be a positive quality. As I probed deeper, Susan recalled lots of happy, fulfilling instances where she led with her empathic, compassionate, sensitive heart. Such an observation caused her to reassess living life according to her dad's beliefs.

Uncovering negative beliefs is harder when they're buried in truthful principles. Jeremy grew up in a household that valued hard work. From the time he could walk, Jeremy was assigned chores and told, "If you want to eat, then you need to work." The middle school baseball coach recognized that Jeremy showed a lot of promise as a pitcher, urging him to try out for the travel baseball team. Jeremy excitedly asked his parents to sign the baseball permission slip. They told him no, that work always comes before play and spring would bring a lot of chores to do around the house. Jeremy funneled his disappointment into his feelings holding tank and incorporated a strong work ethic lifestyle.

Reaping the benefits of that belief, Jeremy graduated college in three years, landed a prestigious job, and put together a financial portfolio most people would envy. But Jeremy could never slow down and smell the roses, never just spend an evening hanging out with his wife. She'd ask him to snuggle on the couch after the baby went to bed and Jeremy would sit there for a few minutes, then remember he needed to fix something or finish a report and walk away.

I asked Jeremy what he was thinking and feeling during those times and he replied, "I don't want to be lazy." We discussed his definition of laziness. I watched the dark cloud over Jeremy lift as he realized God had a different definition. He now had permission to embrace God's truth rather than continuing to live out the model taught by his parents. Character qualities are directly related to heart attitude and motives, not only actions. Jeremy still values hard work and teaches his son how it feels to do something well. But he also understands loving ourselves and others well sometimes looks like going fishing!

The beliefs we have about ourselves are directly related to the values in the culture around us. Parents, churches, ethnicities, geography, etc. all play a part in the messages we receive about our character. As children, we absorb these values and incorporate them into our life. In adulthood, we need to critique them, asking God to separate the wheat from the chaff. The Apostle Paul talks about the differences in faith and individual beliefs in Romans 14.

> The man who eats everything must not look down on him who does not, and the man who does not eat everything must not condemn the man who does, for God has accepted him. Who are you to judge someone else's servant? To his own master he stands or falls. And he will stand, for the Lord is able to make him stand. Romans 14:2-4 NIV.

This entire chapter urges us as individuals to seek God's truth for our own lives, rather than adopting a set of beliefs created by someone else. One major purpose in writing this book is to give you permission to truthfully see yourself. Hearing directly from God helps you live the life He wants for you. People and institutions that demand total adherence to one set of beliefs while judging others are exactly the people Paul was writing against in Romans 14.

Pressure to conform usually comes in the form of comparison. Comparison is an insidious, destructive tool utilized to undermine personhood. There's a difference between looking at someone as an inspiring, illustrative model and using comparison to demean and hate ourselves. Kids who watch Olympic athletes or find their science

teacher amazing can use those models to spur on their own achievements. Parents who compare siblings to each other or to other children wound souls.

Advertisements negatively compare skinny weaklings to strong
muscular guys, giving the impression gals only care about muscles.
While we cognitively believe there's more to life than looks, money,
prestige, etc., we can still find ourselves automatically making negative comparisons because of our culture's worldview. God's enemy
loves when we discount our own personhood and focus on others,
rather than embracing our own qualities.

Once I decide to do something, I want to dig in, keep moving, and
get to the end. I feel good about that quality. I've always been inter-
nally motivated with a lot of patience and perseverance. Those are
great qualities in some circumstances. But when there's a barrier I
can't seem to get past, I've tended in the past to beat myself up about
my inadequacies by looking at others who I judge to be more successful. Each time I went through that cycle, it was harder to see myself
truthfully.

I could see that same pattern in how I approached difficult relationships, when I looked at my finances, how I felt like a bad mom, a
sinful Christian, and how I had terrible self-care habits. Adopting a
drill sergeant mentality, I would look around at others and use the
negative comparisons to push me to change. Sometimes it kept me
motivated for a whole week. Other times I landed in despair after a
few hours. Many clients have utilized this strategy successfully, using
guilt and negativity to achieve weight loss, gain respect, or make it
through a difficult circumstance. The cost to their personhood, however, is enormous.

In my early 20s I began to gain weight and I've struggled with it
ever since. Like most women, I've spent a bunch of money on diets,
gyms, trainers, special foods, doctors, supplements, the latest fads, etc.

I put my internal motivation in overdrive and was determined I'd be like the little engine who could and make it up the mountain. As usual, that only lasted a short time and I ended up in a pit of condemnation at the bottom of the hill. Hating myself for not achieving my goals, I was confused as to why all my efforts, intentions, and willpower failed. I doubted myself, becoming reluctant to take risks in all areas of life. That was one of the driving forces behind my decision to go see a counselor 16 years ago. I couldn't find me underneath all my incorrect beliefs and negative strategies.

At 54 years old, I've now lost 75 pounds and 10 dress sizes over the past four years. My trainer says I work out like an athlete! I still have 40 pounds to lose, but my approach is so much different. Not only was my body burdened by fat, it was primarily burdened with beliefs that were not true about me and how God wanted me to live my life. Throwing off the lies and embracing my own uniqueness, I've been able to harness the motivation and energy to do the positive things to be healthy.

Beliefs About Others

Isn't it amazing how the messages we received from significant people in our childhood still affect our present? What rules are you still believing/obeying?

- ○ Always use the crosswalk
- ○ Make sure you wear clean underwear in case you're in an accident
- ○ Parents/authority figures are always right
- ○ Pastors/church leaders always know what God wants for every individual's life
- ○ You have to be nice to everyone
- ○ Always put others before yourself
- ○ Anger is sinful
- ○ You should always make your bed

○   Eat all your food because there are starving children in
Africa

Look at all the things you have to feel guilty about! You'd be sur-
prised at how many of the beliefs and messages we ingested as a child
negatively impact our adult life. I always felt that my mother believed
she knew better than me about everything. Whenever I had an idea
or did a task, she would offer another solution or tell me how she
would do it differently. I'm sure my mother would say her intention
was to help me, but the message I received was that I was always
wrong. Being a stubborn gal, I would go into defense mode when I
heard the message that I was wrong or incompetent. Hence the fax
machine war!

The information we receive from others either limits or expands
our ability to love God, ourselves, and others. For many Christians,
they have a belief that loving everyone the way God does means they
have no choice but to play nice with everyone -- no matter how it
harms them personally. I encourage you to critique that belief. In
wrestling through it for myself, I know I'll be unable to love or care
for anyone if I don't have permission to recognize when people drain
me physically and emotionally. Jesus was in contact with God every
second he was on earth, but even he became overwhelmed by the
needs of others and the heaviness of life, needing to step away to re-
fresh himself.

Messages from Dad and Mom

One of the benefits of colleagues working in the same office is the
opportunity to share insights. Mark and I have talked a lot about the
differences between men and women pertaining to relationship roles,
emotional needs, and maturity processes. I know some folks bristle at

the idea of stereotyping genders, but social science research has always confirmed common gender differences.

God loves us in ways that nurture us in both masculine and feminine forms, because He is all and everything, lacking nothing. As humans, we obviously cannot encapsulate every quality of God in one person. So God created both male and female human beings. It takes both the unique masculine and feminine traits, viewpoints, and skills to raise children well. Ideally, as parents live out their own personhood, they model to their children how to love God, themselves, and others within the context of a family. When parents have received a poor model themselves, their ability to meet their own children's emotional and relational needs is compromised.

The Mature Love Model below shows the need for parents to move out of their comfort zone to support, encourage, and facilitate needs for the parts of their children where they do not overlap. Child 1's comfort zone overlaps significantly with the parent, so it's easy for the parent to nurture that child. But the overlap with Child 3 is minimal. If the parent does not make the effort to move into that child's life, wounding will take place. The transformative process helps us get healing for our own immaturities, brokenness, and burdens which become barriers to sacrificial love.

Mature Love Model

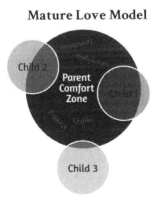

Human fathers provide an experiential picture of how God the Father sees us and feels about us, forming the basis of how we look at ourselves. When human fathers stay within their own comfort zone without validating their child's personhood, kids get the message that if I'm different, it means I'm wrong. This belief then gets projected onto God, making it hard to believe God likes those different parts of us as well. Children instinctively believe their mother will always love and support them. But children know dad will be truthful; he doesn't have to like or love them, so dad's words and actions are often more impactful.

Sons look to their father to be a life model. They watch the balance between work and play, relationship and individuality, selfishness and caring. When a father's goal is to recreate themselves through their son, the child becomes an object to be used for personal gratification rather than an individual to be respected. If a son makes it his mission to "make my dad proud," other important things in life won't be prioritized leading to relational dysfunction.

My conversations with Mark have shown there are three important areas where fathers significantly impact their daughters. To the extent fathers fail to do these well, daughters are left with gaping holes in their self-esteem leading to unhealthy relational choices.

○ *Fathers need to validate their daughter's world.* Most little girls see their dad as a respected man who does important grown-up things at work. They love their mom for being loving, caring, and making great cookies, but getting dad's approval is essential. What message is she getting if dad always sits in his easy chair, asking his daughter to please play with her dolls in the other room because he's watching sports? What about the dad who agrees to have a "spa day" with his little girl, loving her giggles as she puts make-up on him and curlers in his hair? Dismissing feminine interests as frivolous and superficial or labeling a daughter as a "drama queen" feels like a slap in the face, making daughters question themselves. When daughters see dads intentionally coming out of their comfort zone into their feminine world, gals value their own personhood.

○ *Fathers need to validate the godly character qualities they see in their daughter.* So often, fathers only give words of approval about completing tasks. They give praise if the child gets high grades and does their chores, give stern lectures about breaking rules, and may even ridicule kids for being emotional. **Humans value tasks, God values people.** Fathers need to see their daughter

through God's eyes, telling her things like what a compassionate heart she has, how proud they are of their daughter's sense of justice, and how they love to see God shine through her. When daughters get the message that only approval comes when they complete specific actions, they will believe God only accepts them when they are "good." Hearing dad say, "I love to see how much you care about animals," makes his daughter feel happy and proud. She'll learn to say, "I really like that about me too!" Embracing our personhood means seeing, accepting, and enjoying the qualities that make us uniquely special in God's eyes.

○ *Fathers need to be proactive in coming alongside their daughter to talk about how they will live out their personhood.* Most fathers talk to their kids about how to become successful in terms of making money, getting a good job, prestige, etc., whatever is important to the father. It's imperative that fathers actively pursue their daughter. Many dads tell me they have an open door policy; their child is welcome to come to them at any time. But if their daughter wants to talk about her feelings, her relationships, or how she feels about her body, dads will usually tell the daughter to talk to mom. But our heavenly Father pursues us. He's always nudging us to talk about our day and how we are growing and maturing.

Fathers need to intentionally seek out their daughter and pursue conversations on topics out of their comfort zone.

Mothers tend to model the caretaking, nurturing side of relationships. Giving their kids a foundation of unconditional love. Being physically and emotionally available to children provides safety and stability in a crazy world. Mothers translate "female speak" to dad on behalf of daughters, so dad has the information to meet their emotional needs. Fathers need to value the softness and caring mothers bring to their sons. I very much appreciate how my ex-husband has always valued the ways I care for Ben that are different from what he brings to the table. We moms need to fuss over our kids sometimes without being told we're coddling them unnecessarily. On the other hand, mothers need to trust the male bonding rituals between dads and sons that take place in ways that often feel scary or look mean to us.

Sons learn how to care for other people and sacrifice their own comfort by watching their mom, understanding how their actions can have an emotional effect on her. That helps them be able to care for their own wife well someday. [Benjamin, honey, if you are reading your mom's book right now, your mother would feel very happy and loved if you would open doors for her when we're on vacation!]

Husbands and Wives

When there are relationship problems, most often the cause is rooted in emotional wounds received in childhood. Many married clients come into the office believing if their spouse would make a few behavioral changes, everything would be fine. When I ask about the relationship models in their own childhood, clients often dismiss any parallels from their family of origin to their marriage.

Research has shown most people marry someone who is very similar to the parent with whom they have the most unresolved issues. Most often, that means gals marry someone who relates to them the same way as dad. And sons eventually recognize mom qualities in their wife. Many times, my clients will be adamant that they married someone completely opposite from their parent. But when we start looking at character qualities rather than individual details, the client ends up seeing many of the same patterns. Other clients immediately admit they married a carbon copy of their parent, but have absolutely no idea why.

Rhonda described her father as rigid and strict, with no patience for excuses. Dad valued hard work and obedience. Her mother was a no nonsense gal who didn't have time for femininity for either herself or her girls. Rhonda married a military man who belittled her when he thought she wasn't working hard enough, becoming verbally abusive when she voiced her own opinions.

As we talked, Rhonda shared how hard she found it now to give herself grace for mistakes, enjoy self-care activities, and even to show her femininity through her wardrobe. The more Rhonda asked God to let her see herself through His eyes, the more she grieved the failures of her parents to love her well. Rhonda's beliefs about her self-worth were instilled by her parents.

These beliefs affected all the major decisions in her life. She unconsciously found a man similar to her father, trying to resolve her own feelings of inadequacy from within the marriage. Rather than grieving the failure of her parents, she put herself in harm's way and became like her mother. Rhonda is learning to process through her feelings to find the beliefs that have kept her personhood prisoner for many years. What decisions she makes about the marriage will come out of conversations with God about his plan for her life.

Luke came to my office to talk about feeling disrespected by his children. His anger with his children caused Luke's wife to become overprotective and their relationship was suffering. When he explained the behaviors that frustrated him, I could see they were developmentally normal, childish sibling actions. When someone makes a mountain out of molehill emotionally, it means there's some sort of emotional trigger to the past. As we talked about his mom, Luke realized she would blame him for her negative feelings and he learned how to put up a defensive wall.

As an adult, it was very difficult for Luke to take responsibility for anything because it felt like he was once again being unfairly blamed. Luke's inner child made a vow that when he became an adult, he would never allow anyone to disrespect him. As a parent, Luke misinterpreted and personalized his own children's' words and actions. Luke now asks his wife to signal him when he needs to step back and process his own emotional reaction to events. I'm very encouraged by his willingness to receive conviction and correction from God.

Beliefs About God

Beliefs about God are rooted in what we've learned about sin. Many church doctrines focus on God's judgment against those who are sinful. Young children form a view of God that convinces them He is waiting to punish them for any wrongdoing. I just flat out don't believe that is true and if Jesus were here, I think he would start turning over a bunch of church pulpits for that blasphemy! How dare anyone teach that God's heart attitude is one of revenge and retribution. Such teaching comes from a jaded, punitive, judgmental system created by humans, not the loving, caring heart of God.

Young writes about this same theological confusion in *The Shack*. The lead character, Mack, is trying to reconcile his picture of an angry, punitive God with the caring entity he's personally experiencing in the shack. Mack views God as someone who enjoys having the power and authority to punish people who disappoint him. Young's response, written from the perspective of God the Father, is very profound.

> *I am not who you think I am, Mackenzie. I don't need to punish people for sin. Sin is its own punishment, devouring you from the inside. It's not my purpose to punish it; it's my joy to cure it. (Young, p. 119-120)*

Reminds me of Jesus standing on the Mount of Olives looking over the city of Jerusalem, saddened by humanity's unloving choices that will bring about horrific pain and destruction. Humans create false beliefs about God and his motives because we cannot or choose not to live connected to God's heart. It's much simpler to create a list of do's and don'ts, say they're from God, then demand everyone follow them. But Romans 14 says God gives truth to each person individually about how to live a godly life. When we're connected to God's heart, we've no need to be worried about failing or disappointing our creator. No matter how many times we mess up, God lovingly picks us up, dusts us off, and teaches us the same lesson over and over with infinite patience.

A Belief-Driven Lifestyle

It's essential that we allow God to critique the beliefs on which we base the foundation of our life. From childhood, we gather information from various sources around us and use it to form our beliefs. Children are concrete thinkers, they take things very literally and tend to view things as black or white. As a result, they come up with beliefs that don't take context and extenuating circumstances into consideration. Children also tend to adopt values and beliefs they hear and see modeled by important people in their life. Like a baby bird swallowing its food whole, kids often parrot beliefs without critiquing the concepts. The Bible tells us to examine our faith so we can give an account for our beliefs. That means we must submit those beliefs to God and hear directly from Him what is true.

When people create their own beliefs and difficulties arise, people will question God's motives rather than re-evaluate their own beliefs. For instance, take the belief about whether God loves us when He doesn't answer our prayers. Most people will give an intellectual answer, but when the unanswered prayer is something important, our own beliefs are uncovered. Do you believe God is good -- always? If truthful, most people will shamefully answer no. The serpent got Adam and Eve to question God's goodness, even in the Garden of Eden. Our own belief is exposed during hardship and trial when we stand back and become God's judge.

Humankind's viewpoint is always based on some type of judgment, because we create an idyllic standard we can't sustain. Matthew 5:48 NIV says, "Be perfect, therefore, as your heavenly Father is perfect." We apply that to mean do more things, follow more rules, beat yourself up about everything, etc. because we judge ourselves and others against a standard we can never achieve. But the perfect thing about God is that He is good and is always working within us for our good. Because we do not truly believe in God's goodness all the time to everyone in all circumstances, then we do not trust him.

> *If you knew I [God] was good and that everything--the means, the ends, and all the processes of individual lives--is all covered by my goodness, then while you might not always understand what I am doing, you would trust me. But you don't. (Young, p. 126)*

What does it look like to live out a lifestyle based on the belief God is good? Think about Shadrach, Meshach, and Abednego. These young boys were taken from their homes and marched off to Babylon where they were put into a training program to serve King Nebuchadnezzar. Before captivity, God planted his heart deep into their souls through the written word, but also through the godly models around them. Even at a young age, these boys had a clear understanding of God and His character. I'm certain many other captives came to the conclusion that God had abandoned them. Becoming bitter, these captives turned away from God, exactly the way many of us do in difficult times. The question of God's goodness in the face of human depravity sends people one of two directions. People either draw closer to God, so they can be comforted by his heart, or they shake their fist at him, judge his motives, and declare their independence.

Tori hung onto the hope God would change her difficult circumstances with the same intensity as hanging on for dear life to a rope suspended over the Grand Canyon. Laid off and unable to find another job, the bills piled up and Tori was panicking. She claimed prosperity in the name of Jesus, telling everyone God would not give her any more than she could handle. Tori desperately wanted God to validate her belief in his goodness so that her entire theological belief system would not crumble. As the foreclosure proceedings took place and the date for the sheriff's sale loomed, Tori's hope faded and she became despondent. Folks around Tori began to sound like Job's friends, saying God was angry with her lack of faith.

When we hang onto a belief about God that is tied to circumstances, our limited understanding sets us up for anger, despair, and hopelessness. When I asked Tori how she felt about God, she replied that God was not who she thought he was any more. That's true, He's not. He's not a sadist who takes pleasure in inflicting pain on others, nor is he only interested in someone learning a lesson by any means. God does not sacrifice one person only to save someone else. While many of you would probably agree with these statements, do you question God when difficulties happen in your life? Unless we are anchored to God's heart and see circumstances through His eyes of love, we end up like Tori, falling into the Grand Canyon.

The account in Daniel shows Shadrach, Meshach, and Abednego's roots were deeply embedded in trusting God, not focused on escaping difficult circumstances. From the beginning, they asked for a diet that kept them physically and spiritually strong and healthy. Daniel 1:20 says the king found them to be 10 times wiser than anyone else in his kingdom. Rather than sitting in despair, asking God to rescue them, they looked for the ways God was blessing them and they prospered. Our definition of prosperity is usually related to the absence of negative circumstances. God has a different definition. Ask the Apostle Paul.

King Nebuchadnezzar decided to demand everyone in the kingdom bow down to a golden statue in his likeness and worship it. Shadrach, Meshach, and Abednego were summoned before the king who insisted they bow or they would be thrown into a furnace. Talk about pressure! Their answer reflects they knew exactly who God was and how he cared for them.

> O Nebuchadnezzar, we do not need to defend ourselves before you in this matter. If we are thrown into the blazing furnace, the God we serve is able to save us from it, and he will rescue us from your hand, O king. But even if he does not, we want you to know, O king, that we will not serve your gods or worship the image of gold you have set up. Daniel 3:16-18 NIV

They expressed understanding of God's power and authority in the situation and also trusted in God's decision whether to act to save them or not. By their declaration, they were resting in the knowledge of God's love for them, separate and apart from human circumstances. The depth of their understanding of God's love and goodness, even as they were being thrown into that furnace, is inspiring. Because of their trust, these Israelites allowed King Nebuchadnezzar an opportunity to see God from their viewpoint, and the king's heart was moved.

Everyday clients talk about not being able to trust important people in their life; especially God. Trust only comes as a result of knowing in our soul that we are loved. Until we really know the truth from the author of love, we cannot give trust to anyone else, especially broken humans.

My process of taking head knowledge and anchoring it into my heart began with making a list of all the fears I had about not being able to trust God. They included things like being afraid God would ask me to go to Africa and be a missionary, that he would take away the things that I loved and replace them with things I hated, that God would tell me to follow all the same rules everyone else did without listening to me, that he would be the boss and I would be a slave who wasn't allow to have a voice, etc. As I looked at my list, I realized all these fears were rooted in wounds I had received from my family and other Christians. My model of God and the way He loved me was based on faulty human beings and I needed to replace those beliefs with truth. That was a big revelation and brought a lot of hope.

I know that in the above account God stepped in and miraculously saved Shadrach, Meshach, and Abednego from harm. Such miracles do not happen for many of us. But the story is not centered on the physical miracle, but the relational bond of trust between the men and God. Every one of us has to choose our own lifestyle based on our beliefs about God. Do we demand the miracle or walk into the furnace to find Jesus there with us? Transformation requires truthful confession of our self-protectiveness, faulty beliefs, need for human approval, and a willing heart to replace them with God's truth. In the next chapter, I explain how to desire truth in your innermost parts.

REFLECTION QUESTIONS

1.   Which beliefs limit your ability to live a joyful life?

2.   Describe how you see yourself and your character qualities.

3.   Do you use "drill sergeant" tactics like comparisons to push yourself to live up to your own or someone else's standards?

4.   What rules are you still believing/obeying from childhood? Do they help or hinder living an adult life?

5.   Do you see parallels between emotional wounds received in childhood and how you interpret present conversations?

6.   What self-esteem messages did you receive from disappointing interactions with your mother/father?

7.   How does your view of sin affect your view of yourself, God, and God's view of you?

8.   What process do you use to actively engage God and allow him to critique your foundational life beliefs?

9.   Are you holding onto pain that has turned into bitterness and resentment toward yourself, others, or God?

10.   Do you find it hard to believe that God is good and loves you well in all circumstances?

CHAPTER 8

Truthful Confession

When my son Ben was 16 years old, his dad generously bought him a used car so he could drive to school, work, and activities. I supplied Ben with a credit card on my account to make sure he had access to emergency funds. A few weeks later, Ben took money out of his savings and drove to his favorite baseball card shop. He bought the first set of cards and unwrapped them at the store, excited to see what gems he uncovered. The store owner took advantage of Ben's enthusiasm, tempting him with the possibility of greater reward if he would just buy a few more sets of cards. Ben justified his actions by telling himself he could pay me back when he got his next paycheck. Twenty minutes and $1,200 later, he maxed out my credit card and terror took over. My phone rang and Ben was in a panic, absolutely distraught, apologizing profusely. Once I got get him to calm down, the entire story tumbled out.

Ben was faced with two choices: hide in fear or move toward relationship. The decision we make comes out of our character. Character is formed by the life strategy we choose. Ben, like King David, understood we all make mistakes and have immaturities in life. Sometimes we act with intention and other times immaturity sneaks up on us. What's important is heart attitude and the courage to truthfully confess our brokenness rather than running from it.

At the moment the machine declined the credit card, Ben felt the weight of his choices. Surrounded by discarded wrappers and piles of baseball cards, Ben's first thought was that he financially ruined me and he couldn't fix it. I love that Ben was grounded in knowing his own character and my heart of love for him in the midst of his immaturity. There was no self-hatred, condemnation, or worry that this event would change our relationship. Such security allowed him to move toward me, acknowledge his actions, express concern for the impact on me, and accept my care for him. Yes, we talked through what he learned about himself and, yes, he did eventually pay back every penny!

How many times have you said or done something that negatively impacted someone else and you still can't forgive yourself? Truthful confession is about agreeing with God about who we are and how He feels about us in our immaturity. We must radically change our view of sin and immaturity in order to believe God loves us unconditionally, that His only motive is to help us grasp that truth more every day. Truthful confession replaces fear of failure, disapproval, and disappointing God and others resulting in gratitude for corrective guidance and freedom.

Loving God and others often requires sacrifice. Most clients believe no one will like them if they show who they are inside. When I dig deeper, the fear is usually based on not wanting to lose a relationship. Living in truth sometimes requires disappointing other people. There's often a crossroads moment where we know in our soul God has asked us to walk out a path or to shine light into darkness and doing so will bring conflict and misunderstanding. This is where our viewpoint is so important. We're called to trust that God will work all things together for the good of both parties if we trust in His direction. The relationship may need to change so God can work in both hearts. Truthful confession means we choose to believe in God's loving motives rather than hiding out of fear.

Freedom Thru Truth

John 8:31-32 NIV makes an extraordinary promise.

> *"To the Jews who had believed him, Jesus said, 'If you hold to my teaching, you are really my disciples. Then you will know the truth, and the truth will set you free.'"*

Freedom is something humans have been fighting for since leaving the Garden of Eden. Freedom from external oppression, slavery, and bondage. Freedom from internal self-doubt, woundedness, and false beliefs. God promises if we draw near to him, bringing our beliefs about ourselves, about God, and the self-protective strategies we have used to survive, He will give us truth and we will be set free. Amazing! I can hear your question, "So how do I do that?" **By choosing principle over protection; relationship over fear.**

By an intentional act of our will, we can choose to align our beliefs with God's truth. My favorite example is the conversation in John 4 between Jesus and the woman at the well. The Samaritan woman had all sorts of beliefs; theological, moral, cultural, socioeconomic, etc. Jesus offered her the opportunity to critique her beliefs through the viewpoint of God's heart rather than human standards.

He pursued her with every question, leaving it up to the woman whether she wanted to move forward or draw back. Each question required her to become even more vulnerable and honest -- and each truthful reply brought her a new level of freedom. As she began to see herself through God's eyes, the Samaritan woman's shame was exposed and she discovered her true personhood. Her destructive choices and immature actions came out of false beliefs about her worth and value. With those lies exposed, she was set free.

The Samaritan woman's freedom began by choosing to risk engaging in conversation with Jesus. She had no clue who he was or if he posed a threat to her. At any point in the conversation she could have shut down and backed away. What kept her engaged? I believe she was captivated by Jesus' transparency and openness. He stepped out of the conventional, cultural box to actively pursue her heart. Each question allowed her to experience more of Jesus' love for her, making it safe for her to let down her guard. Believing in God's heart allowed the Samaritan woman to find freedom through truth.

Agreeing with God

I've always been that stubborn person who refuses to believe anyone or accept anything unless I wrestled it through for myself. Such a trait can make it very challenging to be in relationship with me. (Remember the fax machine standoff!) Part of that is my hardwiring; character traits God instilled in me as part of my personhood. Other times, such stubbornness comes out of past woundedness, fearing I still don't have permission to have a differing opinion. Being able to see ourselves clearly, strengths and weaknesses, allows us to quickly agree with God and spend less time wrestling.

A healthy, transformed lifestyle means we have permission to put all of our thoughts, words, and actions out on the table and have a conversation with God without worry of rejection. I've been so privileged to see how this permission has significantly impacted my life and the lives of so many of my clients.

My dad always called me stubborn because I refused to believe someone just because they were my parent, teacher, or pastor. I may have agreed with them, but the lack of permission to decide for myself generally made me become unreasonable and angry. Once I grasped the truth that I had permission to wrestle with God, my self-defeating behaviors subsided and I found that God and I actually agreed on a lot of things!

I began meeting with Rory after she was released from the hospital for swallowing a bottle of pills and cutting her wrists. This sad, angry teenager talked about feeling like a lost, blind person searching for her identity in a dark room. Rory had no voice in her own life; just a series of demands placed on her by others. Light began to penetrate Rory's despair when she risked sharing with me her hopes and dreams. I didn't have an agenda, didn't put pressure on her to do something or believe in anything. I just sat and marveled at Rory's vulnerability and saw God's image in her uniqueness. It makes me cry to think about how this beautiful, delicate flower opened up and learned how to receive care from me which, in turn, allowed her to believe in a God who loved and cared about her. Rory is now a vibrant, passionate gal who sees herself truthfully and has been empowered to take up space in the room rather than living as a wallflower.

The teenager in me loves how Jesus' lifestyle and teachings got the establishment up in arms. He was seen as a radical extremist because he viewed the world through God's eyes rather than humankind's conventions. Sometimes we need to step out of our box in order to challenge our beliefs. I think Jesus asked folks a lot of "why" questions about beliefs and practices they took for granted. The Pharisees set up a trap for Jesus in John 8 when they brought him a woman caught in adultery. Using an outcome-based view, they thought they had trapped him into agreeing with them based on the law. But Jesus simply ignored their attempts, reframing the entire event by questioning their motives and character. I absolutely love that response!

I, too, look for opportunities and resources to help me step out of my box. William Young's book, *The Shack*, is one of the most profound books I've ever read. What I find so captivating is the unconventional approach Young took in portraying each person of the trinity. There was a big outcry by many mainstream traditional churches at picturing God the Father as a large African-American woman who called herself Papa. Many thought it was sacrilegious to put Jesus in jeans and work boots and to portray the Holy Spirit as an Asian ethereal sunbeam. Because the characters were so different, I personally paid a whole lot more attention to what they said and did rather than skimming over theological concepts I'd heard a million times.

This story wrestles with the concept of understanding God's heart of love in the midst of unthinkable tragedy. Young offers readers an opportunity to view this concept by putting us in a different role, thereby giving us a different viewpoint and the ability to understand God's heart more fully. Young's transparency allows access to his thoughts, feelings, and opinions, facilitating individual discussions with God about his true nature.

Mack is given the opportunity to sit in the judgment seat and is asked to judge God and the human race. He rants about all the pain inflicted on innocent victims by broken, immature people, saying God should punish them so they feel the same pain. In response, God shows how Mack's own children are immature and cause hurt and pain to themselves and others. Mack is told he has to choose two of his own children to be sent to hell for their actions. While agreeing his children are not perfect, Mack cannot conceive of sending any child to hell. Realizing a choice must be made, Mack breaks down and begs God to allow him to take the place of his children. At that point Mack is able to conceptualize God's relationship with each and every human being.

You have judged them worthy of love, even if it cost you everything. That is how Jesus loves. (Young, p. 163)

The courage to ask deep, probing questions gave me insights into God's heart for myself. I, too, have asked God why he allows so much suffering. Stepping out of the "why" box to look at the world through God's heart has changed my entire viewpoint on life. I can now see that once the relational connection to God was broken through Adam and Eve, humans had to come up with their own system for teaching people to love one another. Being disconnected from God allows selfishness to take hold of hearts. The fact that God mercifully saved Cain's life after killing his brother shows the difference between the punitive, judging system set up by humans. Jesus was outraged at how the merchants at the temple took advantage of people, but he still loved them dearly. Being able to love people so much that you are frustrated with them not living out their potential is a difficult concept for humans. We want to either love someone completely all the time or hate them forever.

It's astonishing how we can be set free, even when our circumstances have not changed. At the end of this story, Mack's children were still immature and as a result, would still hurt others, sometimes even intentionally. Mack still hated people being wounded and hated the brokenness within people that allowed them to hurt others. But he moved from being a judge to being a father, and that relational connection changed his viewpoint and his heart. That's what it looks like to choose principle over protection; relationship over fear, and align our beliefs with God's truth.

Truth in the Midst of a Storm

Anxiety is one of the strongest barriers to living in truth. When folks are worried and anxious, their primary goal is to find relief at any cost. According to *the Anxiety and Depression Association of America*, anxiety disorders affect 40 million adults (18% of the U.S. population). Anxiety disorders have a physiological component where the brain incorrectly analyzes threat information due to a chemical imbalance. But there's also a learned component involving avoidance. If anxiety was primarily due to a chemical issue, medication would solve the problem. Since millions continue to suffer with anxiety, even on medication, I believe there's a deeper issue that fuels the anxiety cycle.

In Luke 8, Jesus fell asleep in a boat as his disciples sailed across the Sea of Galilee. A storm came up and the boat was in danger of being swamped by water. As the disciples looked at the waves and felt the fear inside of them, their ability to see truth decreased. Panicked, they woke Jesus up claiming they were on the verge of drowning. Jesus did an assessment and rebuked the storm. He then asked the disciples, *"Where is your faith?"* I don't think he was chastising them for having worry and fear. He was, however, pointing out how they allowed fear to isolate them from God.

Faith is about a person and the disciples tried to handle the difficult circumstances in their own strength. God doesn't always promise to immediately rebuke the anxiety storm in our life, but he does promise to give us strength and truth when we bring him into the situation. We see Peter's growth in understanding Jesus' message when he later walked on water towards Jesus, only sinking when he focused on his fear.

Holding onto truth when our emotions are on high alert is hugely daunting. When panic sets in, we equate feeling with truth, believing *"If I feel this much fear about something, then my worry must be true. If my worry is true, then I absolutely, must, always do whatever relieves the anxiety."* Truth cannot enter into this equation. We put our belief in truth by an act of our will based on trust in a person. **When we separate**

truth from God's heart, we do not have the courage and emotional energy to withstand the anxiety storm.

Anxiety and fear-based protective thinking and behaviors run the spectrum. It ranges from a few jitters before giving a speech to having such an inability to manage anxiety and normal life risks that a person cannot leave their home. It's my belief there is always an emotional component in any level of anxiety. One of my specialty counseling areas is Obsessive Compulsive Disorder. Most people think the main issue with OCD are all the odd things people do or think like worrying about germs or having to check the stove a bunch of times. In actuality, having OCD is like being held captive by horrendous aliens in a terrifying sci-fi movie laboratory.

It's a horrific hell of never-ending intrusive thoughts causing overwhelming emotional terror by convincing the sufferer that something horribly catastrophic is/will happen to them or someone they love. I've talked to new mothers who are terrified they will put something dangerous in their baby's bottle by mistake. If they don't know for certain they've focused 100% on each step of making the formula, they throw out the batch and remake it, even when the baby is crying from hunger. Other moms constantly worry their children will get sick so they hover over them, sanitizing wipes in hand and deny requests to go to friend's houses.

Kevin turned himself into the police station one evening, telling the officer he couldn't stop worrying he might stab his wife in the middle of the night. He had no history of ever hurting anyone, but Kevin was so worried he might act on it that he wanted to be locked up for the safety of his family. Regina watches the news every night, certain there will be a story about a hit and run matching her car's description. She retraces her drive to and from work numerous times to make sure she didn't hit a pedestrian. Sometimes it takes Regina more than three hours to make the 5 mile trip home from work. Most people would listen to these worries and dismiss them as unreasonable. But to someone suffering from OCD, just the fact that the thought crossed their mind tells them they are guilty. Fear that something terrible could have taken place generally trumps logic, reason, and even incontrovertible evidence that the client did nothing wrong.

The leading treatment for any anxiety-based diagnosis is Cognitive Behavioral Therapy (CBT). The premise is that if a person is exposed to their fears long enough, the brain will re-learn how to correctly analyze the threat and the anxiety will go down and not return. It's seen as a simple reprogramming of the brain. Exposure Response Prevention (ERP) therapy asks the client to create a hierarchy of the fears based on the level of anxiety they experience. The client is confronted with those fears starting with the least anxiety-provoking to highest.

I do see the value of CBT and ERP, but they completely leave out the emotions in the holding tank that generally fuel the worries. Learning how to touch a "contaminated" doorknob is helpful, but it's completely divorced from the underlying emotional triggers that fueled the anxiety in the first place. As a result, the anxiety will return when the client is exhausted and can't muster up the energy to do ERP. Unfortunately, clients will usually become discouraged, believing they aren't strong enough to overcome their anxiety.

Sandy always wanted to be a preschool teacher. She loved kids and was excited to finish her degree in Elementary Education. During her first classroom internship, Sandy began having intrusive thoughts that she was touching the children inappropriately. Every night she'd replay every event of the day, viewing each interaction frame by frame. The anxiety became overwhelming as she worried about how she touched the children and whether she had wrong motives when interacting with them. Eventually she had to take a leave of absence from school because she was so fearful that she was a pedophile.

Sandy spent three weeks attending an intensive outpatient CBT/ERP clinical program. Participants created a fear hierarchy and were required to go out in public and do odd behaviors, things they felt were "dangerous" and would lead to "catastrophic harm." Clients have shared how humiliating these types of ERP sessions felt. They've told me that although they may have made some behavioral progress, their self-esteem plummeted. Sandy was asked to go to a mall playground, watch the kids play, and intentionally imagine touching them inappropriately. The next week she was asked to imagine approaching parents at the playground, telling them she had impure thoughts about their child. The goal of this exercise was for her brain to be able to separate out an active choice vs. an intrusive thought. Sandy understood the need to reprogram the brain and by the end of her intensive treatment, she was able to deal with the worries more effectively. But the ERP experience was devastating. The embarrassment and shame Sandy felt for deliberately engaging in these actions cemented the belief she was "crazy."

Sandy returned to school and successfully got her degree, but her joy was gone and everyday was hard. During our first session, Sandy briefly reported being sexually molested when she was very young. She denied any long-term effect, saying she hadn't thought about it in years. As we talked about the feelings holding tank, her Child part began to come to the surface. Over the next weeks she was able to release the pain she had stored up and came to a truthful understanding of her own character. Sandy continues to intermittently get anxious thoughts, but she calls on God to help her stand firm against the storm.

The way I approach OCD and anxiety-based symptoms is to encourage clients to acknowledge their feelings of helplessness. How do they feel knowing they can't control people and circumstances to keep themselves and others safe? It's not just a rational, cognitive acknowledgement from which you move on to make behavioral changes. Learning how to dig down to the underground river of feelings and allowing yourself to feel truthful emotions lowers the obsessive worry water table. I believe the largest fuel source for anxiety is found in the underground river we create when we cannot/do not directly process through our feelings in a relational way.

Usually when clients walk in my door, they've felt isolated and "crazy" for a long time and have very little hope that I can offer them anything different. Their families are frustrated with their worries and personalize it when the client won't just believe them. Traditional therapy believes in a problem-solving approach. It tells families to stop giving reassurance and to refuse to go along with anxiety-based requests. The client feels isolated and even more anxious. This approach creates an enormous amount of tension in the family. It applies a system that was made to fix problems -- not meet emotional and relational needs.

When a child is frightened, whether due to an actual or imagined fear, the instinctive parental response is to comfort and reassure the child they are safe and not alone. Once reassured, most children are able to get clarity on what is and isn't true. Why should it be any different for those of us who suffer with anxiety? I ask spouses to view it as a little child who's worried they're facing something too big for them and they feel all alone. Stand with your spouse and make a united front against the anxiety. As the client drinks in the experience of not being alone in their anxiety-filled hell, they get stronger and have more ability to bring clarity and truth into situations.

Sherry had constant worries about her health. When her heart beat fast, she thought she might be having a heart attack. When there was a bruise on her arm, she thought it was bone cancer. Every time she had a physical worry, she begged her doctor to do every conceivable test to rule out all the catastrophic possibilities. The time and money invested in her health concerns were overwhelming. Her husband was frustrated at the situation, yet wanted to love his wife well. Rather than immediately having her go through traditional exposure therapy, I spent time understanding Sherry's family background and relational dynamics. Sherry shared how she tried to always be "good" so her parents didn't worry about her like they did her siblings. When she did let her needs be known, Sherry was generally disappointed because her parents just patted her on the head and told her to run along so they could work.

Her lonely cries went unmet unless she created some type of drama. This unconscious strategy continued into adulthood and began to threaten her marriage. Sherry spent time grieving the failure of her parents to see and address her God-given core longings and emotional needs. Grief allows us to pour out all of the resentment and bitterness that builds up when we don't process disappointment. Grieving allowed her to move past the emotionally neglected child she had been to embrace a vision of a healthy, strong, caring woman, wife and mother. Only then was she ready to tackle the anxiety.

Sherry chose to step out and risk her physical welfare. She gave her husband a letter stating she was trusting in his decision making regarding how to approach her physical complaints. Sherry then wrote a list of truths about God and her husband so she would have something tangible to remember when anxiety struck. I got the first panicked phone call from Sherry when she was on vacation.

> "I've been having headaches for two days. I looked on WebMD and I'm sure it's a brain tumor. I desperately want to go to the nearest ER and have the doctors run all the tests."

> "What does your husband think," I asked.

"We talked about my symptoms and he says we should wait to see how I feel when we get home this weekend."

"How do you feel about his decision, Sherry?"

"I want to believe he's taking this seriously, but a big part of me thinks he just doesn't want to ruin his vacation time. I know that doesn't sound true, but I just want to feel better now, no matter what it takes."

We continued to talk about her list of what was true about her husband's heart. Sherry agreed if she chose to go to the ER against his advice, she'd continue the old pattern of agreeing with anxiety rather than with God. By the end of the phone call, Sherry bravely decided she wanted to trust in her husband's heart. When put in relational terms, Sherry saw the choice was between self-protection and trusting in his love and care for her. Choosing self-protection kept her in an isolated, anxious hell. Potentially dying from an undiagnosed brain tumor seemed like a worthwhile risk to take in order to receive a life based on truth.

When I spoke to her the next day, Sherry told me she felt sad she couldn't immediately appease her anxiety. Although the "what ifs" continued to haunt her, Sherry acknowledged feeling empowered. Choosing to stand on principle rather than being pushed into something she later regretted strengthened her view of herself. These days, she continues to get the "what ifs," but Sherry knows to head straight for the loving arms of her Heavenly Father, husband, and children rather than her MD!

Truth in Sorrow

Truth is also about coming to an acceptance of reality and allowing ourselves to grieve what we wanted to be true. Grieving is an essential skill in the healing process. Seeing truth, whether about ourselves or others, usually brings a time of sorrow. God designed us to mourn together, drawing encouragement and strength when we're emotionally vulnerable. Rather than funneling feelings into the holding tank, the grieving process validates loss and its effect on your life so you can learn from it and use that information to move forward.

Many years ago I read a very insightful book about the grief process called *Hinds Feet on High Places* by Hannah Hurnard. It's an allegory based on The Song of Songs. The Chief Shepherd promises Much Afraid she can live in the Kingdom of Love with him forever if she undertakes the transformative journey from her home in the Valley of Humiliation.

Before she can start on her journey, the Chief Shepherd says he must plant the seed of love in her heart. Looking at the seed, she sees it has very sharp corners and Much Afraid asks if it will be painful. The Chief Shepherd explains that love and pain go together while here on earth and to have love, she must accept times of disappointment and pain. This was her first pivotal crossroad. Would Much Afraid choose self-protection over vulnerability? This is the same question each one of us must answer.

We count the cost of where we are now in life and decide whether our self-protective strategies are heading us toward the abundant, joyful life we want to live. The Bible promises that loving God, ourselves, and others is the key, but the cost is learning to allow sorrow, disappointment, and grief into our life. We cannot choose to stay isolated and self-protected from pain and be able to love well. One or the other must be sacrificed. Jesus, a man of sorrow and acquainted with grief, loved much and grieved well.

When Much Afraid reaches the foot of the mountains, the Chief Shepherd introduces her to traveling companions Sorrow and Suffering. The Chief Shepherd lovingly asks her to trust in his motives. He urges her to embrace Sorrow and Suffering as companions in this present world, promising they will lead her to a deeper ability to love well. We, too, wish the healing journey could be walked in the company of joy and peace, often becoming angry, bitter, and afraid when circumstances are difficult. Viewpoint is so important. Do we move toward God's heart in difficult times or away in fear?

Elizabeth Prentiss was married to a clergyman in New York City. In 1856 two of her children died and she questioned God about why he let this tragedy happen. She chose to move forward, sharing her sorrow, finding truth. As a result of her wrestling, she penned a hymn that is still sung today.

More love to Thee, O Christ, more love to Thee!
Hear now the prayer I make on bended knee.
This is my earnest plea; More love, O Christ, to Thee.
More love to Thee, more love to Thee.
Let sorrow do its work, come grief or pain;
Sweet are Thy messengers; sweet their refrain.
When they can sing with me; More love, O Christ, to Thee.
More love to Thee, more love to Thee.

Most of us look at these words and wonder how we could ever feel this same way in such tragic circumstances. They key is to understand that God also feels the same sorrow and grief we feel. Understanding that truth, we can mourn with Him and receive His comfort and solace. Otherwise, we feel isolated, abandoned, angry, and bitter. The Bible recounts many times when David ran for his life from King Saul. At those times, he would honestly pour out his heart to God so he could receive truth and comfort.

As Much-Afraid made her way over the mountains, she encountered several of her Fearing relatives. Pride tried to convince her the

Chief Shepherd did not have her best interests at heart. Pride told Much Afraid she was opening herself up to ridicule and embarrassment by taking a different path from those around her. Much Afraid held the hands of her companions and stood firm against anxiety.

For quite a while, Much-Afraid was able to trust in the path laid out by the Chief Shepherd. She then found herself on the Sea of Loneliness and was assaulted by Resentment and Bitterness. Resentment told her how unloving the Chief Shepherd was being to her, making her walk all this way through such hardships. He told Much Afraid to demand the Chief Shepherd fulfill his promise immediately and take her to his kingdom. Bitterness pointed out how the Chief Shepherd took everything of value from her. He advised Much Afraid to run away so the Chief Shepherd didn't continue to take advantage of her. Then Self Pity chimed in, crying how unfair it was that Much Afraid had given so much and tried so hard and she didn't seem to get anywhere. He told her he felt sad the Chief Shepherd delighted in making Much Afraid suffer. The poor gal was exhausted being surrounded by her Fearing relatives day after day.

Much-Afraid asked the Chief Shepherd how these relatives had gotten so close to her at this point in the journey. He showed how impatience had grown in her heart. Even when we believe God is leading us to greener pastures, we can become weary and exhausted of walking out hard things every day. That's when these voices fill our ears and we question God's heart towards us. Being able to recognize we are camped at the Sea of Loneliness allows us to ask God to send people to care for us until we are refreshed.

I Kings 18 tells the account of Elijah on Mount Carmel challenging Ahab & Jezebel's prophets of Baal to a contest of power. After an all-day showdown, Elijah prayed one prayer and God showed himself to be real. Afterwards, Jezebel declares she's going to kill Elijah for destroying her prophets. 1 Kings 19:3 says Elijah became afraid and ran for his life. He goes into the desert, lays under a tree, and asks God to take his life because he feels like a failure.

Elijah was listening to the Family of Fearing. He had expended himself doing work for the Lord and was vulnerable to depressive thoughts and inaccurate beliefs. Rather than a rebuke, God sent an angel to strengthen Elijah so he could continue on his journey. Once again, truth is delivered through the vehicle of love.

Heaven is our home, but we're not living in heaven yet, we're still on the journey. Along the way we will have times where we're exhausted from burdens of hurt, pain, and caring for others, causing us to step outside of God's heart. That's when we doubt God's intentions. Like Peter who stepped out onto the Sea of Galilee and got distracted by the storm, we need to refocus and return to relationship. Grieving allows God and others to bear our heavy burdens so we can find hope in the morning.

Freedom is attainable. Trust me. I've been on the anxiety side, gone through the Valley of the Shadow of Death, and now I'm praising God, eating at the banqueting table, and helping others make the same journey. Whether you find yourself stuck in anxiety, disappointment, grief, or confusion, your heart can be set free. The next chapter paints a picture of freedom in Christ.

I am still confident of this: I will see the goodness of the Lord in the land of the living. Wait for the Lord; be strong and take heart and wait for the Lord. Psalm 27:13-14 NIV

REFLECTION QUESTIONS

1.   How secure do you feel in God's love and acceptance of you, even in the midst of your immaturity?

2.   What role does fear play in your life and relationships?

3.   How does shame keep you enslaved to a fear-based life?

4. Is it more difficult to forgive yourself or to receive forgiveness from God and others?

5. Do you have permission to wrestle with God by talking about the hurt, pain, and disappointments in your life?

6. In what areas of your life do you choose self-protection over trusting in God's love for you?

7. How does anxiety or "what ifs" impact your life and decisions?

8. What does it feel like to have Suffering and Sorrow be part of your life?

9. Do you see evidence of Resentment, Bitterness, or Self-Pity in your heart?

10. What burdens do you need to grieve through so you can have hope in the morning?

CHAPTER 9

Living Free

You've made it through the valley of woundedness, liberated your feelings from captivity, wrestled your inaccurate beliefs into submission, planted your flag on the mountain of truth, and now you're ready to live free! Of course, life's always a journey and you'll be back on this road when another wound comes to the surface, but now you know what to do.

I feel very strongly in process. Mark makes fun of my business cards that say, "Healing is a journey of discovery," but we both wholeheartedly believe in process. I see learning and process all through the Bible and in real life examples. Process equips us to learn something through the mess of today that will help us navigate a difficult hurdle tomorrow.

Writing this book has been an amazing process. Releasing it into your hands as a reader is an uncomfortable, scary prospect because you'll have all sorts of reactions and feelings to my personal disclosures and counseling concepts. And yet I've taken the risk.

Living free is all about trust.

Trusting in a God who loves us extravagantly and intimately at the same time. Trusting in ourselves as an amazingly unique creation whom we give as a gift to the world. Trusting in God to give us wisdom in surrounding us with people who can love us well. I so hope you are as excited about this life adventure as I am!

In this chapter I share a few tools I've found helpful in living a prospering lifestyle. Living free is energized by clarity and vision; clarity about God, ourselves, and others and vision to see how God can use our personhood in meaningful ways. No longer weighed down by fear of disappointment, you can dream big and risk boldly.

Seeing Yourself Clearly

Most folks live a "follower" lifestyle dedicated to keeping others happy, getting approval, following the rules, being obedient, etc. When clients choose to live in truth, they first have to learn what is true about them! Every day, clients tell me they don't even know who they are nor where to start figuring it out. It's like putting together a complicated puzzle without having a picture on the box. The goal is to see yourself the way God sees you, embracing your uniqueness, living out of your strengths, identifying your weaknesses, and having permission to love yourself just the way you are today. I utilize three tools to gather information: Spotlight, Feedback, and Hardwiring.

Spotlight

Ty is a single guy in his mid-30s with depression symptoms. During our initial session, Ty had a hard time meeting my eyes and answering my questions. As I gathered information about his childhood, it became obvious that Ty was not used to being in the spotlight. He kept asking if he was "doing it right" and if he was "giving me the answer I was looking for." Not surprisingly, Ty described himself as being very insecure, self-conscious, and said he preferred being in the background.

When he came for his second session, I asked Ty how he felt about our first meeting. "Weird," he answered. "Different than what I thought it would be like." I asked Ty what he had expected. He thought I would be like a medical doctor telling him what was wrong and providing some tips on how to fix things. What he experienced was being asked by a stranger to expose all the parts of him he'd been trying to hide for 30 years. Ty chose to come back on a regular basis, knowing he would still feel uncomfortable in the spotlight for a time, recognizing he needed to experience being seen if he wanted to change.

I have another client named Denise who's a huge extrovert. She walks into a room full of strangers, delighted she's going to make a whole new group of friends. On the surface, Denise seems very comfortable being in the spotlight and sharing stories about her life. But I notice she always deflects my attempts to dig deeper, to be pursued below her comfort zone. When I pointed this out, Denise shamefully confessed she "talked a good talk," but was actually very insecure and uncertain about her personhood.

Being seen is a scary risk. Putting aside the masks, self-protective strategies, and roles to be seen at your core is often terrifying. It's much easier to make behavioral changes than to allow yourself to be seen by God and other people. Being seen means risking others seeing things we don't like about ourselves. Fear blackmails us into shutting off a part of us that God wants to heal. Taking the step to be seen and choosing to interact with safe people moves us along in the transformative journey.

Feedback

Receiving feedback from others is generally how we've been wounded. The negative messages we received as a child caused us to develop our self-protective mechanisms in the first place. The Bible says healing only takes place within relationship. Learning to process our emotions and critique our beliefs strengthens personhood (relationship with ourselves). We need to embrace permission to own and experience our opinions, thoughts, and feelings and ask God to bring safe, caring people to bring into our life.

Christina was the seventh child out of 10 kids. Mom ran the home like a drill sergeant. Getting kids out of bed for school, food on the table, and household chores done required everyone to play their role. Life at home was focused on efficiency and practicality. When she was eight years old, Christina excitedly won the part of Mary in the church Christmas play. Christina felt like the belle of the ball standing on stage during the first rehearsal. As the family drove home, Christina happily asked her father what he thought of her performance. He replied, *"You are causing your mother a lot of trouble. We don't have time to drive all over town in this weather. All you're going to do is stand there. Why do you have to go to rehearsals for that?"* She was crushed and vowed never to ask for feedback from anyone again. Unfortunately, this was neither the first nor the last time Christina received hurtful comments motivated by selfishness.

Christina has worked hard to empty resentment and bitterness stored in her emotional holding tank over the past 42 years. Like David, she's taken aim at her Goliath-size beliefs that no one is to be trusted and she will never be safe sharing anything personal. Christina now has a small network of friends and she's intentionally allowing herself to be in the spotlight by asking for support, encouragement, and giving her friends permission to speak into her life.

When the feedback we've received has come from unloving hearts, we automatically shut ourselves off from others. Being able to receive feedback from God and others gives us valuable clues as to who we are at our core. We all have blind spots about ourselves that can only be revealed by permitting others to see us and share their observations. The first thing you do when putting a puzzle together is to turn all the pieces over so you can figure out how they fit together. Allowing input from God and others, even if it feels uncomfortable, gives us a clearer picture of ourselves.

Hardwiring

Understanding hardwiring gives context to the automatic ways we think, feel, and act. There are many different personality tests that can help you learn more about your hardwiring. I've found the *Keirsey Temperament Sorter* to be very helpful in identifying strengths, understanding coping mechanisms, and interpreting emotions.

As an Intuitive, I've a very complicated way of gathering and putting information together. It's based on inspiration, hunches, and gut instinct -- so trying to explain in this book how I got to my beliefs has been a huge challenge! When I was a kid, I had a hard time explaining what I knew. It was like trying to show all the work in a math problem when you "just knew" the answer. Now, this is the quality I love most about my personality because it's my way of communicating with God all day long.

I was a litigation paralegal for many years prior to going to graduate school for counseling. My employers loved my quirky mind because I would make all these odd connections when I was working on cases. Once I was searching for a man who owed our client some money. He'd disappeared and our client didn't know where the debtor was living. I searched online records including court records, recorder of deeds information, and licensing board information in numerous counties. My mind works like those pop ups on your computer. They lead you one place and you get a flash, so you go a different direction and get another little nugget of information sending, you down a different trail. Crazy process, but I usually find something important – and I found the debtor! Questions come through my mind all the time, which you can obviously see as you've read through this book! It's through these "I wonder" thoughts that I believe God guides me while interacting with clients.

Understanding your strengths and weaknesses in the context of hardwiring helps give perspective. If God created you to view the world in a particular way, then embrace it, celebrate it, and don't let the enemy tell you that being like someone else is "right" or "godlier." God has purposely given each of us a unique mind, body, heart, and soul to enjoy ourselves and care for others. Nurturing those qualities brings thankfulness for how God made us.

I was part of a year-long women's Bible study a few years ago. My co-leader and I had opposite hardwiring, but those differences allowed us to bring something of value to each member of the group. I felt very blessed that my co-leader (whose name also happened to be Judy!), was strong in the areas I was weak. Resting in her unique care-giving allowed me to focus on what I brought to the table. Respecting the personality differences in others instead of demanding they change allows us celebrate God's handiwork.

Don't Settle for Better, Reach for Great

Whenever fear is the motivating factor, it causes all sorts of problems. Looking back over my life, I lived a predominantly fear-based lifestyle. I ran every idea and decision through an internal grid, asking how much anxiety it would cost me. Many people live a model focused on keeping the negative out. The motto is, "don't take risks that could either bring problems or cause disappointment." Problem with that thinking is you're aiming for status quo and survival, not reaching for healthy and prospering. It's much harder to strive for a happy, joyful, abundant life than settling for not losing what you have.

The Roadmap to Freedom transformative process I've laid out prioritizes working on the foundational aspects of life. It's like taking a lot of time digging out dirt and installing the cinder block basement to be sure it's built sturdy and plumb. You don't really see much change until you begin building the framework of the house. Most of the time we just want to FEEL better quickly and sacrifice doing the foundational work to BE better in the long run. Take a look at the model below and decide where you are today.

Folks who've grown up in a chaotic household, surviving through neglect, abuse, addictions, mental illnesses, etc., focus on the Survive Life strategy. The only goal is to keep your head down, stay out of trouble, and to remain intact physically, emotionally, spiritually, and mentally.

Once this child grows to adulthood, they crave a Safe Life. A Safe Life prioritizes keeping the really bad stuff away so the client can feel safe and secure. Fear is still the enemy, so they'll avoid any type of conflict that could lead to feeling helpless and unsafe. This person will accept blame and responsibility if it quickly brings back a sense of safety. This explains why women continue to live in abusive relationships. Such a client will tell me how their current situation is much better than what they experienced as a child. The desperate need for feeling safe outweighs the cost of living with an abuser. Believing they may never find another man who will put up their issues, this fearful gal will justify and rationalize an abuser's actions so she can maintain the illusion of safety.

Living a Manage Life strategy focuses on security -- hanging on to what you have rather than risking disappointment or failure in striving for something better. I lived in this category for many years, making decisions based on what I had to lose rather than what I had to gain. The belief in this household is "good enough is good enough." If you want more than the status quo, others will tell you what you stand to lose if you spend money, time, effort and energy on something that might not work out. Risk is characterized as unreasonable and illogical.

Abigail grew up with a father who suffered from Bipolar Disorder. When in his manic phase, he was full of giant plans for the future, talking about changing the world with his ideas. Dad made his boss angry by criticizing management and he'd get fired. Full of enthusiasm, Dad took Abigail on spending sprees, putting down payments on expensive cars, buying her piles of toys, and making extravagant promises. On returning home, Mom and Dad would get in a big argument about finances. Feeling guilty, Abigail couldn't even take her new toys out of the bag. Several times they packed up their stuff in the middle of the night and left their apartment, skipping out on the rent payment. When Dad was in his depressed phase, he sat in the living room watching TV all day long in his underwear. He barely talked to Abigail when she spoke to him. Mom's patience would wear thin and Abigail did her best to quickly do her chores so she could escape to her room.

When Abigail graduated high school, she took a job in a big chain department store on the other side of town. After working for six months, she was able to afford a tiny apartment and moved out on her own. Abigail was a diligent worker, following every instruction given by her manager, making sure there was no reason why they could find fault with her work and dismiss her. She created an organized, dependable lifestyle by living modestly and not taking any risks. Abigail's store manager promoted her several times over the next few years and her dedication was recognized in the corporate office. When a high level administrative position opened up in Chicago, Abigail was offered the job -- which she turned down.

Over the next five years Abigail was offered several other job transfers, but she turned them all down. Now approaching her 30th birthday, Abigail sat on my couch wondering why she wasn't happy with her life. We talked about her priorities and she began to see that although she gave herself a safe, secure existence, she wasn't really living a proactive, engaged life. Taking a job transfer meant risk, financial expense, and uncertainty. She'd learned to fear all the things required to pursue an adventurous lifestyle. Abigail needed to choose whether she wanted to continue living the Manage Life strategy or choose to live a Great Life.

Living a Great Life is rooted in growth.

God is always giving us opportunities to grow in loving Him, ourselves, and others. This strategy requires keeping your eyes on the horizon, anticipating the blessings and opportunities God allows in your life. Growth comes in the form of evaluating whether each opportunity fits into your season of life and learning how to wisely take risks.

Do you ever watch the daytime TV show called *"Let's Make a Deal?"* Monty Hall used to be the host and now it's hosted by Wayne Brady. I know this because I watch the show almost every day and I'm fascinated by the decision-making of the contestants. The host offers the person a choice between two potential prizes. Many times, one of the prizes is a sure thing and the other is unknown. It's so interesting to see the folks who immediately grab the revealed prize, as if they're afraid it'll be taken away from them. Then you see the contestant who gives up $500 for a chance at a new car, saying they came with nothing and they want to take a chance on winning big. Even when they end up with a zonk, they still feel really great about taking the chance. I want to live that kind of life. Sure, I'd be happy with $500 (and I know I have permission to make either decision), but I'm excited to consider all the unknown possibilities behind Curtain 2! Focusing on not screwing up just makes us more paranoid about the possibility of getting it wrong. The Apostle Paul talked about pressing forward, running the race, being all that you can be (well, maybe he didn't exactly use those words!). His imagery was not about tentativeness, self-protection, or fear. He was bold, daring, and not afraid to be shipwrecked!

I love to see God's hand in the opportunities that come across my desk. Whether or not they actually come to fruition is less important than pursuing a lifestyle of putting myself out there to risk disappointment while hoping for joy. When fear and anxiety surround me, I revert back to the Manage Life or even Safe Life strategies. Those who love me allow me to vent my fears, pull out the false beliefs, remind me of truth, and paint a vision of the Great Life God wants for me.

Name Change

Names are very important in the Bible, a foreshadowing of character. God symbolically changed names when folks came through their wounded valley journey into His promised land of truth. One of the most impressive changes was self-centered, immature Jacob whom God renamed Israel. I believe God speaks a new name to each one of us when we reach this final stage in our transformative journey. The Israelites set up Ebenezer stones to remind them where God had done great deeds and spoken powerful words. Meditating on the new name God has shared validates the long, hard transformative journey and ignites excitement about the future God has in store for me.

In Hannah Hurnard's story, *Hinds Feet in High Places*, the Chief Shepherd promises Much Afraid he will change her name when she reaches his kingdom. After a long, exhausting journey, Much Afraid's heart leaped for joy as the Kingdom of Love was revealed at the top of the next hill with the rising of the sun. She began running, anticipating reaching the kingdom quickly. The closer she came to the mountain, the more forbidding it appeared. Steep, sheer rock faces with an impassable precipice that only deer could climb. Much Afraid broke down in tears as Craven Fear tormented her, gruesomely sharing all the ways she could be injured on such a path. Her companions, Sorrow and Suffering, begged Much Afraid to call for the Chief Shepherd. She could not do so, terrified he would require something impossible of her.

When the Chief Shepherd came to check on her, Much Afraid told him she decided she didn't really want to be given hinds feet to climb the high places. He laughed, saying he knew her better than she knew herself. Of course she still wanted to grow and mature, she was just focusing on fear instead of believing in his power to transform her weaknesses. The Chief Shepherd told Much Afraid a person cannot see themselves differently until they face their own fears and beliefs.

Much Afraid gathered her courage and crossed Mount Injury while holding onto Forgiveness. Her Fearing relatives returned to confuse and derail her in the Forest of Danger and Tribulation. The Chief Shepherd encouraged Much Afraid to travel in trust rather than fear. She refused to allow Craven Fear to paint a negative picture on the screen of her imagination.

Sorrow and Suffering helped Much Afraid to the edge of the Falls of Abandonment. Trusting fully, she stepped off the cliff and landed in the arms of the Chief Shepherd. When she awoke, Much Afraid found she had, indeed, been given wonderfully powerful hinds feet to skip over the hills. The Chief Shepherd had transformed into the King of Love. He joyfully pronounced her new name as Grace & Glory. Overflowing with thankfulness, Grace & Glory turned to her companions, finding they had changed as well. The King of Love explained that Sorrow and Suffering change to Peace and Joy when we embrace them in our journey to God's heart.

Walking out this transformative journey to freedom brings internal contentment and external congruency. My self-talk is dramatically different as I live out of the new name God has given me. Very seldom do I beat myself up with condemning, unkind thoughts. I've worked on seeing myself the way God sees me. I'm now able to be compassionate and loving towards myself when I'm fearful or immature, because that's how God responds to me.

Seeing Life Through the Lens of Relationship

I was complaining to a friend one day that I didn't feel comfortable with my dentist. She asked why I didn't find a new one. The question stumped me. As I journaled, I realized I often looked at people as service providers rather than relationships. I just picked the hairdresser, dentist, banker, doctor, etc. who was most convenient and made it work. Only many times it wasn't working -- hence the complaining! I hadn't put a lot of thought into who would be a good resource to support me. It was a gigantic light bulb moment to realize that from God's viewpoint, I needed to look at everyone in my life through a relational lens.

So I went back and looked at how I felt about my dentist. I felt comfortable with the staff and the dentist was very thorough. For some reason, hearing this particular dentist tell me I didn't brush or floss often enough made me feel like I was in the principal's office. He wasn't unkind or mean, but everything about him made me feel like a misbehaving child. I contrasted this relationship with the most recent dental appointment. The dentist's recently licensed son did my cleaning because his dad was out of the office that day. I enjoyed the son's humor and easy going approach. He mentioned the same things his dad had said, but in an off-hand, FYI, kind of way. It felt like a peer to peer interaction that was a win-win for both of us.

As I described what I figured out to my girlfriend, she said it sounded like the son was a better fit for me. Once again, a huge light bulb moment! I'd never been given permission to acknowledge a relationship was not a good fit for me. What I'd been told and saw modeled was that you were stuck with people and you just had to make the best of it. Many of my clients grew up with this same message.

You know you don't really enjoy being around someone, but believe it's your Christian duty to like them, or at least be "nice." Clients who were taught being nice is a Christian requirement look at me suspiciously when I say there's no verse in the Bible that says we have to be "nice" to everyone. Jesus showed us there's a big difference between loving someone as a human being and wanting to be in a close relationship with them. He loved the Pharisees, even when calling them names. One of the ways Jesus showed love to the Pharisees was taking the time to offer them truth and insight. But his love for Mary, Martha, and Lazarus was shown by establishing a close, intimate relationship.

Having permission to decide whether another person is a good fit relationally validates our ability to have our own individual experience of others and determine whether our needs overlap. God didn't creates us as one-size-fits-all people, so it makes sense we'll all have different needs that are filled by different relationships.

Okay, so I have permission to decide my dentist's son is a better fit for me, but now I panic because I don't know whether my dentist believes in this permission thing! I literally journaled for weeks about how anxious I was to call the office and ask to transfer care to the son, fearful I would hurt feelings. I'd write a bravado type journal entry one day, stating my new belief that God was okay with me asking for what I needed. The next day there'd be tear stains on my pages as I worried the entire dental office would condemn me for being selfish.

As my next appointment approached, the more I journaled, cementing into my soul the freedom God was giving me to love myself by choosing the dentist relationship that was a good fit. I let my friend know I'd be calling the office the next day, just to have a little accountability! I dialed the office and told the receptionist I felt more comfortable with the son and asked if I could switch my care. She answered, "Oh sure, lots of our patients switch between the dentists." I hung up and slapped myself in the forehead like I forgot to have a V-8! Picking myself up off the floor, I was ready to courageously look at more areas of my life that were a mess and needed to be cleaned up.

It was very frustrating to see that although I was healthier in the present, I still had a huge mound of baggage from my past that keeping me in chains. Although I could now create more accurate plans to address the issues, the length of time it would take to dig out from under the pile seemed interminable. I wasn't sure I had the stamina to run the marathon. That was the next important skill I learned, how to stay the course.

At the beginning of my journey I spent a lot of time grieving over the loss of the person I wanted to be, terrified of finding out who I actually was. The time came, however, when I had to make the choice; stay where I was or take the leap. Funny enough, once I made my mind up to find out who I was no matter what, those character traits I thought I'd lost resurfaced. Instead of beating myself up about the

Tim Horton's donuts I'd just eaten, I began to trace my decision-making back to the emotions that started my binge. It became apparent that if I learned how to process emotions directly, I probably wouldn't be stopping for donuts. When I felt unappreciated at work, I used the "I deserve it" excuse to eat something that would anesthetize the pain. Allowing myself to feel the mad/sad feelings in the present gave God the opportunity to open up past times when I'd felt lonely, uncared for, and unappreciated. I learned how to bring God into those memories and feelings and receive the comfort I was craving.

Once I began paying attention to my emotional triggers, the next skill I learned was to not freak out at seeing what a mess my life was in. I'd used the "I don't really want to know how bad my finances are" avoidance strategy for quite a while. When I gathered up my courage to look at the black and white facts, it was really scary. I wanted to stick my head back in the sand, all the while calling myself names and feeling hopeless to fix it all. My counselor told me to just keep taking deep breaths and remind myself it was not always going to be this scary to face life head on. When I became emotionally overwhelmed (which I knew was happening because I so desperately wanted that donut!), I sought out the people in my life who would speak God's words of love to encourage me. With my emotional tank filled back up, I was able to get clarity about what was true and what actions and decisions I needed to take next.

My client Sophia was dejected looking at her unfocused, unproductive life. She'd be all gung-ho about a project or goal for a short while but when she hit a difficult patch, she would just give up. When I asked why she thought that happened, Sophia answered she must be lazy and have no willpower. Humm, doesn't that negativity sound familiar to us all? If we don't know why we can't make something work, we usually blame ourselves. But before you go and slap a big old negative label on your chest, it makes sense to consider what you know about your character and heart motivation. There might be other culprits.

I asked Sophia to look at herself through a relational lens (versus a negative, critical lens) and tell me what kind of person she was. She talked about being a first string college athlete, how she loved volunteering with the children's ministry at church, and confessed she needed the approval of others to believe in her own worth and value. Sophia agreed that the terms "lazy" and "unmotivated" were probably not consistent with what was normally true about her. I then asked if there was a difference in her ability to press into difficulties based on whether it was a goal she was passionate about versus an obligation. Bingo. As we talked, it became apparent Sophia had more success when the project came out of her excitement, passions and visions. With this understanding, we reviewed her plans, goals, and relationships based on the freedom she felt in pursuing each one. As Sophia gave herself permission to decide what was and was not a good fit for her season of life, the heaviness and despair began to lift. She was excited to direct her resources towards the people and activities that were meaningful to her and she was able to stay the course.

Joyful Living

Several years ago I was part of a small musical band with some folks from my church. We'd often go to a food pantry to help feed the homeless and then do a concert. There was a petite, white-haired grandma who loved to play an old, out of tune upright piano as everyone ate their dinner. She'd play hymns and always ask me to sing along. I absolutely love to sing and can harmonize to anything by ear. I'm certainly not a recording artist, but singing has always been second nature for me, like breathing. Each time I came, she'd take my hand, look me in the eyes, and tell me I sang like an angel.

A couple years after I left the band, I was driving down the street and out of the blue I was reminded of her comment. At that moment I heard God's voice in my spirit telling me that I did, indeed, have the voice of an angel. He shared that an angel chose to give her voice to me because she so loved the heart of worship God had created in me. Wow, remembering that always brings back goose bumps! This is where God spoke to me my new name. God uses that memory to remind me what is really true when shame threatens to tell me lies.

Every day we choose which direction we travel on our journey. The amount of progress we make is less important than the choice to keep persevering, in faith, believing that God is always working everything together for good. Believe in God's timing. He will open up our hurt and pain compartments when we're ready to receive healing. I've traveled this road many times and although each time it's hard, I look forward to the transformation that will take place.

Joyful living is not living in denial of pain and hardship, but in anticipation and hope based on the truth of God's character. Cherish the Ebenezer stones in your past, the symbols of where you have seen God at work in your life. Use them as motivation to keep your eyes on Jesus to see what miracles He will perform in your life today.

Living free looks like riding through life in an old VW minivan fueled by thanksgiving and joy, excited to see what's over the next hill. I pray this Roadmap to Freedom will bring you to a place where you are certain of God's love for you, that you really like who you are, and you're excited about your new ability to love others well. Embrace this life adventure and look for me in heaven. I'll be the short redhead directing the angel choir in singing the Hallelujah chorus!

REFLECTION QUESTIONS

1. What value do you see in viewing life as a process?

2. Do you feel uncomfortable being seen?

3. What's your initial response when someone offers you constructive feedback?

4. How does your individual hardwiring/personality help you understand your strengths and weaknesses?

5. Are you settling for good, letting anxiety keep you from reaching for great?

6. How does fear keep you from taking risks?

7. Has God given you a vision of living free with a new name?

8. What relationships are not a good fit for you?

9. How empty/full is your emotional tank?

10. What does joyful living look like for you?

I Long For Jesus

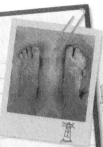

I long to look into the eyes of He who died
for me. To see the love that shines therein
for all eternity. Your piercing gaze into my
heart will cut through my every wall. And
I will gladly surrender to you my hands,
my heart, my all.

Jesus, I long to touch your face, to caress each and every line.
To feel the nail prints in your hands; the punishment that should've
been mine. I want to wash your feet, my Lord, with tears of joy
and love. My heart is longing to be with you in your temple in
heaven above.

Jesus, I long to hear your voice, into my ear you will say The
words I long to hear the most, "Beloved, here you will stay. Forever
you will sit with me, forever by my side. It was only because of my
love for you that I went to the cross and died."

So each and every day of life I struggle to carry my cross.
And sometimes it threatens to crush me and I think that all is lost.
But then I raise my eyes to the sky and pray that soon will be, the
day that I will truly look into the eyes of He who died for me.

References

Anxiety and Depression Association of America. (2014, April). Retrieved from https://www.adaa.org/about-adaa/press-room/facts-statistics

Ben-Shahar, T. (2007). *Happier.* McGraw-Hill.

Bruckheimer, e. a. (2004). The Amazing Race 6. Hollywood, CA: CBS.

Burnett, M. (2004). The Apprentice. New York, NY: NBC.

Carey, H. (1790). God Save the Queen.

Daniels, e. a. (2005). The Office. Hollywood, CA: NBC.

Erikson, E. (1950). *Childhood and Society.* New York, NY: Norton.

Fuller, S. (2002). American Idol. Hollywood, CA: Fox.

Geisel, T. (1954). *Horton Hears a Who!* Random House.

Hurnard, H. (1955). *Hinds' Feet on High Places.* Christian Literature Crusade.

Keirsey, D. (1998). *Please Understand Me II.* Prometheus Nemesis Book Co.

Key, F. (1814). The Star Spangled Banner.

Kid, S. (2002). *The Secret Lives of Bees.* New York, NY: Penguin Books.

Lear, N. (1971). All in the Family. Hollywood, CA: CBS.

Lee, S. (1996). *The Incredible Hulk.* Marvel Entertainment.

Let's Make a Deal. (1963). Stefan Hatos-Monty Hall Productions.

Lewis, C. (1950). *Chronicles of Narnia.* HarperCollins.

Lewis, C. (1952). *The Voyage of the Dawn Treader.* HarperCollins.

New International Version Holy Bible. (1986). Grand Rapids: Zondervan.

Prentiss, E. (1882). More Love to Thee.

Runaway Bride. (1999). Paramount Pictures.

The Lion, Witch and the Wardrobe. (2006). Walt Disney
    Productions.
The Matrix. (1999). Warner Brothers Pictures.
Young, W. (2007). *The Shack*. Newbury Park, CA: Windblown Media,
    Hachette Book Group USA.

Made in the USA
Charleston, SC
24 June 2014